PENGUIN

HENRIE

'This immensely entertaining autobiography has a double value: as authentic social history (giving an insider's view of Soho Bohemia in the 1950s and upper-class hippiedom in the succeeding decades) and as the vivid self-portrait of an unusual and intriguing personality. Neither apologetic nor complacent, Henrietta Moraes describes the vicissitudes of an adventurous and dangerous life with spontaneous candour and unpretentious eloquence. The result is funny, troubling, moving – and impossible to put down' – Francis Wyndam

'She is a natural writer ... her autobiography is lucid, comic ... and has a kind of innocence' – Tim Hilton in the *Independent on Sunday*

'The most compelling autobiography this year. It is also an absorbingly vivid account of bohemian life over the past four decades' – *Tatler*

'An autobiography of amazing clarity and humour' – Kate Bernard in *Harpers and Queen*

'*Henrietta* is a particular pleasure because it is well written ... Henrietta Moraes is one of the most courageous women I have ever come across' – Jeffrey Bernard in the *Daily Telegraph*

ABOUT THE AUTHOR

Henrietta Moraes lives in a room in Chelsea with her beloved dog, Max.

Henrietta

HENRIETTA MORAES

PENGUIN BOOKS

PENGUIN BOOKS

Published by the Penguin Group
Penguin Books Ltd, 27 Wrights Lane, London W8 5TZ, England
Penguin Books USA Inc., 375 Hudson Street, New York, New York 10014, USA
Penguin Books Australia Ltd, Ringwood, Victoria, Australia
Penguin Books Canada Ltd, 10 Alcorn Avenue, Toronto, Ontario, Canada M4V 3B2
Penguin Books (NZ) Ltd, 182–190 Wairau Road, Auckland 10, New Zealand

Penguin Books Ltd, Registered Offices: Harmondsworth, Middlesex, England

First published by Hamish Hamilton 1994
Published in Penguin Books 1995
1 3 5 7 9 10 8 6 4 2

Printed in England by Clays Ltd, St Ives plc

For Joshua and Caroline

*To Deborah for starting me off
and Martha for making me finish*

Chapter One

I was christened Audrey Wendy Abbott in 1931. My father, whom I can't remember ever having seen, was in the Indian Air Force and he had red hair. I've seen one photograph of him. He looked like a fox and he was called Ginger. He tried to strangle my mother when she was pregnant and then took off to parts unknown and was never seen again. I am an only child. When I was young I wanted to find him very much, and when I was eighteen I entertained specific fantasies about meeting in the Hyde Park Hotel and told everyone that I had done so. It was complete fabrication, I just wanted it to happen. I used to think that when I found him my opening words would be, 'You owe me a hell of a lot of pocket money.' But it never happened and I don't know what he was really like at all.

My grandmother used to tell me about my father and she didn't have a good word to say for him, which used to make me very uncomfortable when I was small, because I identified one half of me with this terrible, monstrous, red-headed creature.

With neither father nor brother, I had no male influence in my early life at all. My mother had a mother and three sisters while her father, who had been in the Indian Civil Service, had been dead for a decade. So I was born into this family of women. I didn't meet a boy till I was five, or a man until I was nine. My grandmother had been left a widow in India – a beautiful black-haired, blue-eyed governess from the Staffordshire potteries, a MacEvoy – with these four daughters to educate. She had a son called Arthur who died in his infancy – poor old Arthur. So she brought up these girls, Norine, Joyce, Joan and Lorna, in Simla by herself, with the help of some money but not much of it. They were very isolated – they didn't have army contacts and were without male protection. My grandfather had rather disgraced himself by the time he died by becoming a Buddhist and the grand master of a Masonic lodge in north India and was accordingly excommunicated by his church. The children were sent to a convent on another Himalayan foothill, the mother superior of which was my great aunt. They led very sheltered lives. I don't know where my mother met my father, it's never been revealed to me. Perhaps it was on a picnic. Anyway they met. She was very young, seventeen. They married, but he left her almost immediately after I was born.

Then they all decided to come back to England. I was eighteen months old. My mother and her sisters became nurses and my grandmother took charge of me. She was about the only person I saw from the time I was two. I spent my time almost entirely alone with her and she became very strange. I have absolutely no memory of India at all and can only suppose that I loved it so much that a deep trauma occurred when I left it.

2

So we came to London and my grandmother bought a house in Collingham Gardens in South Kensington. My first visual memory is of walking into this house with a black-and-white-tiled marble hallway, down the steps to the drawing-room and through the French windows into the garden, where I could hear some dogs barking at the other end and a voice saying, 'Down, Mr Bone, I tell you, down, sir.' It was the voice of somebody that I met much later on in my life when he was sixty-four and I was travelling slowly round England with some friends and a lot of horses, carts, wagons and dogs.

I suppose my grandmother was unable to look after somebody so young. She bought a smaller house in Forest Hill in south London and sent me as a boarder to a convent school in Peckham Rye. I was three years old. I wasn't baptized a Catholic but I was suddenly plunged into this convent in Peckham Rye. There are various things I can remember about it. The first is the night that the Crystal Palace burnt down. I looked out of my dormitory window and the sky was absolutely red and fiery.

I must have been extremely frightened and repressed because I remember going to bed one night and being sick all over my bed. I was so frightened of the nuns that I ate it up again, like a little dog, every single bit, and managed to keep it down the second time. I had a little friend – I can't remember what her name was, perhaps it was Pamela. Anyway, she had fair hair and we used to rock ourselves. I suppose it was a form of masturbation. Anyway, it made us feel incredibly comfortable. We used to go around rubbing ourselves. On my fifth birthday my grandmother sent me a chocolate cake which she had made and I asked my best friends to share it with me at

3

teatime. It tasted disgusting. She had baked it with salt instead of sugar and I suffered my first acute social embarrassment. We were never allowed to become entirely naked and took our baths in immense cotton garments, gathered at the neck with string and under which we painfully washed ourselves. We were not allowed to whistle or cross our legs; it was said to cause the Holy Mother to blush. Neither were we allowed to leave any food on our plates. I spent many afternoons staring at unwanted plates of cold fat and tapioca pudding, longing for release but unable to compromise.

At about this time I developed an enormous passion for dancing. I thought I was a ballet dancer, though I suppose I was more like Isadora Duncan. In my grandmother's house I used to turn on the radio and dance for hours and hours and hours and hours. I made friends with the little boy next door, he was the son of a dentist and his name was Robin. I loved him very much and I used to tell him I loved him. 'I love you.' And once he kissed me.

Once I made an attempt to run away and chalked a message on the steps of the French windows, but by the time I had reached the end of the garden I had forgotten all about it. I was astonished by the behaviour of my grandmother, who grabbed me around the neck and chastised me for my ingratitude. I had been quite fond of her, as anyone young would be of the person who gave sustenance, but she was very severe. She used to wash my hair every Friday night and scrub and scrub my head and rinse it in vinegar and then give me a dose of senna pods.

I didn't see my mother very often. She was being a nurse in St Thomas's Hospital. She used to come and see me occasionally and I thought she was absolutely wonderful. I called her 'Mummy Judy', and she was always dressed in black. I don't know how often I saw her. Not often. I think I was something she didn't feel too responsible for, probably because she resented my father's disappearance. She was very young.

I had a scooter. I used to scoot on the roads around the house. I became quite adept at scooting. I used to go along with one leg high in the air behind me and perform all sorts of tricks on it, a trick scooter kid.

I was nine when the war was declared. I remember hearing the announcement on the radio and feeling rather strange and awed. That night there was an air-raid warning and my grandmother panicked completely and made us both go and sit in the cellar with our gas masks on. Mine was a child's gas mask, a sort of Mickey Mouse one, and hers wasn't, and we sat there for what seemed to be absolutely hours. Then the all-clear sounded and we went upstairs again.

My grandmother decided that London wasn't going to be a very safe place to be in and so she bought a house in Bedford. She knew no one in Bedford at all. I can't remember her ever seeing anybody, or ever doing anything except a bit of gardening and a bit of cooking, at which she wasn't very good because she was accustomed to having a lot of Indian servants; so that aspect didn't offer much joy. One of the things my grandmother did do, ritualistically, was to go for a walk every afternoon. There is a river in Bedford called the Ouse, almost always in flood. We used to walk alongside it every afternoon for two hours or so. What I most remember about it was her talking to me about my father. I would ask her what my father was like. She would reply that he was an absolute monster, a really wicked man, and then elaborate on this. Of course I would shut my mind because it was so confusing to me. At about this time something very odd started happening to my grandmother. She became extremely violent towards me. She had always been rather severe but now she was really violent, so I reacted like this: I went to Bedford Modern School for a bit but I didn't make any friends there; instead, I made friends in peculiar places. I made friends with the butcher's boy, he became my friend and so did all of his mates. I had a bicycle and we used to bike to a mill pond called Cardington Mill, which had a wonderful deep pool. I'd learned to swim and I was rather good at it, and we used to spend afternoons swimming there. I can't remember quite how I made friends with the butcher's boy, but before this happened every time I met a boy in the street I used to blush all over my body in the most fierce sort of way. I didn't know what boys were, so I used to have an incredibly strong reaction and flush and blush and turn bright purple.

But when I made friends with all these boys, that stopped happening and they adopted me as a sort of mascot. They were all much older than me, about fourteen; my favourite, Trevor, was sixteen. We used to go swimming and bicycling all the time, and that was very nice, but it meant that I disappeared from my grandmother's house for hours on end, which she hated and she took to punishing me brutally. She got completely out of hand. She used to tie my hands behind my back with a piece of rope and shove me into another room in the dark and leave me there, saying, 'I'm going to come back and punish you.' Much later she would come back with a leather strap from a trunk and lay into me. I used to be covered in these huge weals and bruises, but I never gave in to her. I never asked her to stop and I never cried, not when she was there, I just let it happen, my pride wouldn't allow me to beg her to stop. I suppose if I had done so, she would have stopped – I obviously didn't know how to handle her at all. I used to go to school and go to gym classes, which were performed in vest and knickers. I would be asked where I got my awful bruises from and would reply that I had fallen out of a tree. I would rather have died than let it be known that my grandmother had caused me discomfort.

One day my mother and her sister – my aunt Lorna, whom I was never fond of – came to visit us. I'd done something or other, probably just absented myself on my bicycle for too long. When they arrived, my grandmother said she was going to beat me. This was my first disillusionment with my mother. My grandmother got a strap, while my aunt and my mother sat down in two chairs. My mother said, I thought very feebly, 'Oh, please don't do it,' and burst into tears and just sat there while it happened. My grandmother really lost her head this time and went too far. My mother finally became hysterical and stopped her, but she had let it take place, which was an enormous outrage to me. This is when, I suppose, I lost faith in her and began actively to dislike my aunt who seemed rather to enjoy the scene. It was my birthday.

I had another aunt called Joyce who married an extremely nice Yorkshireman called Stirk. He was the head of transport in Nottinghamshire and kept all the wartime communications open in the Midlands. She wasn't at all admired by her sisters or her mother, but she liked me very much and she was my godmother. She was the only sympathetic person in my family. She sometimes used to ask me to stay with her. My grandmother was so sadistic and extraordinary that she'd wait till the morning that I was supposed to go, come into my bedroom and say, 'Oh, I've had a letter from Joyce. It's all off, she can't have you, you can't go.' My heart would sink and my stomach would churn up. She'd see how upset I was and then roar with laughter and say, 'I only made that up because I know you mind so much.'

Anyway, I went to stay with my aunt Jo after all and I told her what had been happening. She was very very shocked and suggested that I should be sent to a convent again, to a boarding school. None of these grown-up people told me what decisions they were making or why. I just told them things and then, sometimes, events changed. We never had a conversation about it. I would speak to my aunt and she would say, 'You mustn't blame your mother,' but in her mind she had obviously decided to do something.

I was sent to a convent in Matlock in Derbyshire, where I was able to indulge in high spirits. I was relieved to be there. I liked to do things like climb down the fire-escape in the middle of the night and walk around the gardens in the moonlight – things that delight the tomboy. I became very good at running and sports, in order to relieve my pent-up feelings – but I attracted trouble. There was a nun with a heavy black moustache who was built like a grenadier guardsman. She was called Sister Mary Regis. She was Irish, they were all Irish boggery in that convent – bog sisters. I had an odd relationship with her, because I realized she hated me but I knew she also fancied me, and I didn't understand what this meant. I knew she felt very passionately about me, so I would always be at my most cold and proud and independent whenever I had any dealings with her. One day I must have infuriated her by being particularly cheeky, in a cold sort of way, and she grabbed my arm and took me down some stone steps to a room with a huge great boiler, in the depths, like a dungeon. To me it was like being in hell. The flames were reflected on the grimy white walls and it seemed all leaping shadows and dark piles of coal and this great old boiler and gigantic nun towering above, spitting and belching. She started an incredible tirade. She said, quiet and deadly, but with vehemence, 'You're the scum of the earth, you are no good, you are totally evil, you belong to the devil and you are the very spawn of the devil.' I just put my chin higher and higher into the air and she eventually wore herself out. I don't know how long it went on for – perhaps twenty minutes. I wouldn't give in to her but it really shocked me, I wasn't prepared for it. I started getting into trouble with everybody, even my friends. I was put into Coventry by my schoolmates and nobody talked to me for about half a term. I wrote to my mother this time and told her about my troubles. I suppose she felt guilty about me and she made an enormous fuss and this nun was sent back to Ireland.

My mother had gone to live in Northamptonshire. She'd become a private nurse and had to look after an old lady called Mrs Capron, who lived in a house near Oundle called South-wick with her five sons, their wives and children and her only daughter, Elaine. Her daughter became attached to my mother and when Mrs Capron got better, she asked my mother to make Southwick her home and live there with her and I was asked to go there in my holidays. I expect my aunt Jo put some pressure on my mother and said, 'You really must look after your own child,' but it must have been the first time that she was actually able to do so.

Chapter Two

I arrived at Southwick when I was eleven, one winter afternoon as it was growing dark. We drove through the heavy, cold countryside, down a steep hill lined with elm trees, through a park and up to a large house. It was totally bewildering to me because it seemed to be full of children dressed in weird clothes and grown-ups running about. What was going on, in fact, was a fancy-dress party. My convent clothes were abandoned and I was dressed up as a little Arab boy with a turban. I don't believe I'd ever been to a party before or even knew what a party meant. I'd never been in a house with a family in it, living their lives together. It wasn't really normal, it was wartime and people's fathers were coming and going, in the army or airforce. All the children were the grandchildren of the woman my mother had been nursing and they called her Grandmère. Her own children called her Mama. George was her eldest son. He was a colonel in the army and married to a woman called Christian. Their children were Rachel, Elizabeth, Bridget and Christopher. Mama's next son, Eric, was a major and had a wife called Jean who loved me at once and I loved her. She was really kind to me, it was she who dressed me as the Arab boy that late afternoon. She really understood my predicament. Jean had two boys called David and Beresford, and David became my very best friend for the next five years or so. Mama's other three sons were Ronald, a minor canon and seldom seen, Dennis, crippled from a shooting accident, and Roderick, lost in his aeroplane over Holland. Dennis, swathed in a dragon-painted satin dressing-gown and supported on two sticks, used to play Beethoven and Chopin each evening and was looked after by his black-haired housekeeper, Mrs Thornton, a verisimilitude of Mrs Danvers.

Southwick was an English country house and maintained its traditions. Its architecture ranged from the twelfth to the eighteenth centuries. It had a library, chapel, crypt and tower, laundry, servants' hall, stables, park, water-garden and lawns. There were tales of spirits who haunted rooms and yew walks. It was lit by oil lamps and candles, which gave credence to these shadowy beings.

My mother's position was somewhat equivocal in this household, I imagine. She became Elaine's secretary. Elaine dressed like a man. She was very fair and slim with large, myopic blue eyes. She had all her clothes made in Savile Row, her shoes made at Lobb, she wore yellow waistcoats and a tie. She'd stopped in the early Thirties somewhere. She had short marcel-waved hair, cut to the jaw-line. She doted on my mother. They slept in rooms with Miss Gill, an old, pensioned-off governess, between them. They were always together, they behaved as if they were newly-weds.

I spent my holidays at Southwick. I adored it. We played at racing demon incessantly, Monopoly and ping-pong often, murder in the dark, cocky-olly in the stableyard, tennis and croquet. We built a tree house reached by a rickety rope ladder and attempted polo on our bicycles. We danced 'The Flowers of Edinburgh', 'Strip the Willow', foursomes and eightsomes, we wrote and performed plays, one masterpiece of seven minutes in which each word began with a W. David and I were instantly absorbed with each other, we moved faster than the others. We shot rats in the stableyard, we stalked Mr Shepherd the vicar thinking he was a German spy. We exchanged basic sexual confidences on the tower roof and in a hollow willow tree.

Suddenly there were thirty evacuees from all over the place: Strawberry Hill, Clapham, Boston and Philadelphia – Southwick was near an American airforce base. We had our meals together in the kitchen, which was vast. Adams the cook, who had just emerged from the local loony bin in Northampton, was very mad. He would sometimes chase us round the kitchen with a knife. We all sat at one table; the evacuees, the land girls and Adams at another.

Elaine began to look after the home farm with the aid of Peter, a young tubercular manager, and my mother, who performed the secretarial duties. They called themselves Snip (my mother), Snap (Elaine) and Snorin' (Peter), and they did their office work in a small study. All the grown-ups used to gather there before lunch and dinner and do a lot of drinking, which fascinated us because we thought, 'Ho, ho, they come out of there much merrier than when they go in.' The empty bottles were kept in the gun room and we started making these incredible drinks. We used to empty all the dregs of gin, whisky, sherry and brandy into one big jug and down the lot. That was how my love of alcohol was born.

★

In 1943 Elaine decided that I should go to a proper school and that convents were no good, so I was sent to Queen Anne's School in Caversham, just outside Reading. I suppose it was a good school, I certainly enjoyed it. Like all those girls' schools, it was run exactly like a boys' public school; there was an enormous emphasis on games rather than learning or any of the feminine arts. We got up at seven, practised lacrosse or cricket from eight to eight-thirty, rushed down the field to chapel to begin the day. There were prefects, and heads of school, and heads of houses and captains of houses; a frightfully competitive spirit reigned between the houses. I became very high-spirited at this time and I was always in trouble. I didn't particularly like or enjoy authority or even respect it, but I found the way round this was to become very good at games and gymnastics. I realized that if you were good at games, you could get away with many transgressions, a blind eye was turned. If you got into the first eleven, you got into a bus on Saturday afternoon and went and trounced Wycombe Abbey or Roedean – anyway, you got out a bit and had a nice tea. I spent five years at that school. I learned how to play the violin, I was in the school orchestra, I was captain of cricket. All this balanced my anti-social behaviour. I used to go to the cinema all the time in Reading, completely forbidden. I saw a film called *Les Enfants du Paradis* sixteen times. I was always on the razor's edge of expulsion.

My house was called Webbe. We were very partisan and fierce. When I first arrived, Webbe didn't win any games and it was rather a despised house. But when I left, we had won everything. My house mistress was wonderful and protected me from everything, she got me out of really bad scrapes. She was called Miss Watson-Smith, Watty-Smith, and she used to read us books on Sunday afternoons. We were allowed to have a picnic supper every Friday night, which was wonderful. We would take it out into the garden, or sit round the fire in our studies. Otherwise we had terrible food: everything was dehydrated – dried eggs, dried potatoes, dried bananas. So we thought we would breed rabbits. We quickly became very callous. We had three does called Twinkle, Winkle and Binkle. We would stand round them crooning, 'My, Winkle, won't your babies make a good stew?' I had a slow-worm called Joe which I wore like a bracelet on my wrist for two summers.

I discovered how to make a hammock, using sailors' knots. When I'd finished it, I hung it right at the top of a chestnut tree in the garden. This was a wonderful escape from everything, I used to take piles of books up there and be blown about while I read. In the end this tree became festooned with hammocks on every available bough, a bizarre sight, a human rookery. We used to play leap-frogging games, building up the bodies, I think the record was thirteen, thirteen little girls screaming with laughter in the spring and summer evenings.

I was always in love with someone or other. My first love was very pure. She was the head of house; she kept poems of T. S. Eliot under her pillow, which I was fond of hugging. When she left school, she became Eliot's secretary and married him, a dedicated life. The esoteric hierarchy of school was based on a state of being called 'cracked', 'crack', 'cracks'. You were 'cracked' on someone when you were little, then in your turn you became a figure for adoration and had a following of young 'cracks', who would carry your sweater out to a match and take your books to and fro and could always be found at the chapel door waiting for the honour of watching you walk

in, blushing and tittering like idiots. Of course people became cracked on each other. I had a somewhat louche girlfriend called Elaine. She was in a different house, so that our meetings were forced to be clandestine; often enough they took place in some friendly lavatory. We would kiss and embrace hotly for as long as we dared. There was a couple called Nancy – big Nancy – and Carlotta. They performed some ritual together and considered themselves to be married; they had one child, invisible to the untrained eye, and they were passionately devoted to each other. Elaine and I thought them extremely glamorous, but in general it was held that they had gone too far. I longed for someone to repeat this experiment with but never moved further than the lavatories.

Academically, my progress was erratic. I was extremely poor at grasping even the simplest mathematical or scientific principle. My brain didn't work in that direction at all, completely blocked. For instance, if a bath would be filled in half an hour with one tap running, how long would it take to fill with both taps running? My answer was always one hour. My maths mistress, Miss Chamberlain, was called Little Po, which may have had an effect on me. By the time I was fourteen or fifteen I'd been advised to throw maths and physics to the winds and I concentrated English, history, divinity, biology, Latin, French and music. I never did any work, hardly at all. Then the year came for me to take my exams. They were then called Oxford and Cambridge universities, not 'O's and 'A's, and I passed them all rather well with credits and distinctions, and so redeemed myself. I stayed a year longer, in the sixth form, and that was a wonderful year. I gave up everything except English, English history and music, which meant that I had enormous amounts of free time. I spent most of it reading omnivorously. That must have been the year that I went to the cinema sixteen times in a fortnight.

I became captain of my house and I was an awful bully. I remember getting little girls into my study and delivering the most terrible, bombastic, tyrannical lectures about their manners, and how disgusting they were and how sick we all felt watching them eating their meals at table. I enjoyed this, but they snivelled and wept.

That summer I won my cricket colours for play in the Fathers' Match: I took seven wickets, clean-bowled Donald Wolfit for a duck and had a bowling average of 2.5. I blossomed, I blossomed in those five years from being a really rather timid, unsure little girl, into somebody who was very sure of herself – anyway who knew how to move around and where to go and what to do, and who laughed a lot and got on very well with nearly everybody.

A somewhat painful and regular occurrence in these five years was the half-termly appearance of my mother and Elaine. Their unique and startling image was in no way dispelled by their habit of drinking large pink gins at the bar of the French Horn, Sonning; while other parents and their progeny quietly sipped tea on the gardened terraces by the river.

Then it was decision time again. What to do next? Life at Southwick had changed, the war was over, David, Beresford and their parents had moved to Leicestershire. Dennis had shot himself through the head, at his own dining-room table in Ireland in the presence of two cardinals and while the port was circulating; Roderick had been shot down in a raid over Holland; the evacuees were dispersed and my mother and Elaine had moved into the home farm a mile and a half away from Southwick.

Elaine was the only farmer in England who managed to end the war with a £28,000 overdraft, everybody else had made a mint. She had a series of incredibly incompetent and bent farm managers, one of whom my aunt Jo married when her first husband died, a move much deplored by all and sundry. The ménage at the home farm was quite different from Southwick, and not nearly so merry. My mother and Elaine had lived together for five years and the honeymoon period had long been over. Northamptonshire was a sticky, stiff, feudalistic county; they were therefore considered to be a scandalous couple and ostracized, thrown ever increasingly into each other's arms. They had a series of very odd servants. The prime minister of Latvia and his wife played the parts of cook and butler for a while. Nobody stayed very long because it was so isolated, one bus a week from Oundle to Southwick, the bus being a mile and a half away. Then there was a land girl called Christine from Yorkshire who was marvellously pretty but a total slut and couldn't cook at all. She was succeeded by a couple of fairies, Howard and Edward, who drank and had fierce rows in the kitchen all day long. My mother and Elaine, who suffered from *folie de grandeur*, liked to live in style and often took off to London where they stayed at the Ritz and managed to spend a lot of money.

By the time I left school, Elaine had become rather cranky. She and Ma drank a lot; they'd knock back four large to enormous pink gins before lunch. Elaine became rather nervous, drinking, dithering and worrying about her overdraft. One of her friends, Maureen, was a doctor and she was consulted for her advice. Complete rest and a vast bottle of paraldehyde, used to calm patients displaying acute restlessness and violent tendencies. There were some incredible scenes when Elaine accused my mother, quite unjustly, of overdosing her and trying to kill her. They used to have a lot of awful rows and both of them would inevitably turn on me.

I spent a lot of my time riding. When I was eleven, I'd been taught to ride on the lawn at Southwick by a martinet called Ivy Oliver. For three weeks I circled around her on the end of a leading rein, mounted on an obstinate and tiny strawberry-coloured pony, arms crossed on my chest, seated on an old blanket, miserably trying to get the feel of the thing. Later on I was given an old hunter called Montgomery and went out with a decrepit and impoverished pack, the Woodland Pytchley.

The deteriorating relationship between my elders made me feel nervous, apprehensive and not entirely at home. My mother was found *in flagrante delicto* on the office floor in the arms of the farm manager, Colley, and the apple cart rocked precariously. I spilt some ink in my bedroom and Elaine came in, looked at the puddle and said, 'You wouldn't have done this in your own house.' This made me feel terrible, terrible, terrible, because then, all over again, I didn't know where I belonged.

Elaine and my mother gave a cocktail party and I was allowed to attend it, my first grown-up party. I was told, very, very firmly, that I musn't drink anything but sherry, but they forgot to suggest a permissible amount. So I made my appearance and started to knock it back, this sherry, about ten glasses of it, and I suddenly began to feel really peculiar and to sway about and had to be led from the room by my mother and Elaine, who suddenly noticed what was going on. We got to the bottom of the stairs when I fell on the floor. I simply could not get up the steps. I felt as if I was made of india-rubber and all around me was receding and melting. Some time later they managed to propel me upstairs to bed, where I lay in extreme misery for three days being sick. Alice, an old land girl who looked after the poultry, came to see me on the fourth day carrying a jug of water mixed with whipped-up egg whites. She forced this down my throat, and I was instantly cured. But I couldn't drink sherry again for about ten years.

That was my first cocktail party.

My old house mistress had a lot of French connections, French being her subject, and she saw to it that I spent six months in France with a large family called du Boullay, who lived in Paris during the winter and summered in a château near Lyons. I had a few duties, I don't know if I performed them very well. The du Boullays were wine and silk merchants, and so their life was rather a pleasant one. They had five children and innumerable aunts, uncles and cousins; the whole family bore the imprint of a violet rose unfolding on the corner of the mouth. The children were infinitely more sophisticated and worldly than anyone I had ever met. They taught me how to jive, Tommy Ladnier and Sidney Bechet. I used to get terribly drunk because there was always lots of wine with meals, wonderful food which I wasn't used to at all. I became very verbose and my French improved enormously.

I had lots of free time in Paris and I used to take the Métro to any stop that attracted me by its name and get off and walk for miles, exploring. I used to walk in the Bois de Boulogne. It was a wonderful autumn with sunny days, blue skies and golden trees. In Lyons there were lots of teenagers and they were much freer than the English, much sexier and spoonier, and a lot of kissing and flirting went on. It was 1949, the year of Dior's new look, and all the girls had lots of pretty dresses. Which was the one thing that was wrong: I didn't have many pretty clothes and all my dresses were too short. But we used to have a very good time, we used to get up and have breakfast and go swimming and then we'd play tennis – for some reason or other I'd never been much good at tennis but that summer I got really good. It was very pretty country around Lyons. There were a lot of improvised occasions called 'surprise parties', one of those silly French things of copying English expressions and using them in the wrong context. We danced away and I got kissed properly. I was teased a lot for being a virgin. I learned how to play Bridge. We used to sit on the terrace looking over the blue hills of the Midi, playing Bridge in French. It was a carefree time, it was all new to me. I didn't know how people behaved, so I just did as I wished, probably the best thing to do anyway.

Chapter Three

I wanted to be an actress, but I couldn't get this ambition
through to anyone. My aunt Jo stepped in again, I think she
paid for my schooling, and unimaginatively suggested that I
should go to a secretarial college. I agreed because I didn't
know what else to do. So off I went to Queen's Secretarial
College, Queensberry Place, South Kensington, SW7. I arrived
there when I was eighteen, not knowing one single person in
London. I couldn't make head or tail of shorthand, at all, ever.
I learned to type quite well. We learned by listening to
records, lovely old ones like, 'The Girl in the Little Green
Hat', Carroll Gibbons, Turner and Layton, typing in time to
music, our typewriter keys shielded by stout black guards and
our hands mechanically producing classic sentences. 'Now is
the time for all good men to come to the aid of the party', and
'The quick brown fox jumped lightly over the hedge'. My
mother sent me £1 a week pocket money, which did not go
very far.

Then one day the telephone rang. It was my old friend

Mary Lyttelton, an old 'crack'. She said, 'Do you want to come to my brother's jazz club?' I said, 'Yes, very much indeed,' and we went to this club which was in a basement at 100 Oxford Street. It was absolutely crammed. It was the time of revivalist jazz, 1950. Humphrey Lyttelton, trumpet, Wally Fawkes, clarinet, George Melly, vocals, belting out 'Dr Jazz' with the Christy Brothers. I went there twice a week, I loved it, it was quite unlike the atmosphere of my secretarial college, which was full of debs and the daughter of the American ambassador, Sharman Douglas. These girls were different from the ones I went to school with, they were rather rich, it was frightfully expensive this secretarial college; Sharman used to come into my bedroom and tell me about going out to lunch at the Palace and how ridiculous Princess Margaret was. One girl particularly interested me, but she didn't become my friend until a few years later. She had the most huge blue eyes I have ever seen, wonderful blonde hair, and her stockings were always coming down. She looked very much how I felt, thoroughly bored by this awful, mysterious shorthand. Her name was Caroline Blackwood who later married Lucian Freud. Eventually I called my daughter after her and she wrote some excellent books. I grasped shorthand to the extent of being able to take it down but could never read it back, so I never got my diploma and my typing speed was abysmal.

Towards the end of the year I met my first boyfriend, at 100 Oxford Street. He was called Vivian Dewhurst, he played the trumpet, lived in Wimbledon, was exceedingly plain and had very smelly feet. He asked me to visit at home, I went and immediately climbed into bed with him because he asked me to. I had no idea at all that people ever hesitated over this question, or didn't do it, or wanted to get married first. I was

quite amoral in the conventional sense. My mother had never talked to me about such things. I didn't have anyone to swap notes with, and I'd never bothered to ask other girls if they did or if they didn't. I found the loss of my virginity quite painless and actually pleasurable. Luckily Vivian was quite a responsible boy and practical. He sent off for a dutch cap at once by post – I don't know how he knew the right size – and instructed me how to use it. It had never in any case crossed my mind that I might become pregnant. I soon slept with most of his friends, I was quite selfish, it never occurred to me that he might mind. My mother sent me some money to buy clothes with, so I got some that I thought were wonderful, black satin dresses and sandals with ankle straps and great wedge heels. I went to Southwick for a weekend dressed in all this splendour. She called me a whore, so I left. Eventually my mother went to South Africa, where she found the brandy and servants very agreeable. She sent me one letter and, although I wrote back, I never heard from her again.

I shared a flat in Roland Gardens, South Kensington, with three girls – Jill, another Caroline, and the third must have had so little personality that I can't recall her name. The rent was a fiver a week. We all had jobs, got for us by the college. I was working for one of the directors of Eyre and Spottiswoode, who had the distinction of publishing the Bible. I was the worst secretary in the world. Being unable to read any of my shorthand dictation back, I was forced to improvise each morning; my letters were a fabricated mess of inaccuracies, smudges and tear drops. One morning I thought to hell with this, and like a somnambulist walked out of the office and into a telephone box and rang up all the art schools I could think of, saying, 'I'm a model looking for work, have you got any?'

23

They all said, 'Figure or head?' When I found out the difference in payment, half a crown to five bob, I settled for figure and started a new career at Camberwell Art School, Heatherley's in Victoria, Kennington Art School near the Oval, and Chelsea Art School in Manresa Road. I got used to this work quite quickly. The first time, standing naked on a platform with lots of pairs of piercing eyes scrutinizing every inch of my body was rather unnerving but I soon became un-selfconscious. One day, feeling a curious itch in my pubic hair, I looked down at my stomach. A grey, many-legged insect was crawling steadily up my navel. I watched it with amazement, moving relentlessly upwards between my breasts, and gave a shriek of horror: crabs.

I was at 100 Oxford Street one night when a huge man with a beard and a nautical air came up to me and asked me to dance. After the dance ended, he turned to me: 'Your long-lost brother is over there and he wants to see you, now.' Intrigued, I looked up and saw a white-faced, pale-eyed medievalist with hammer-toes waiting expectantly. It was love and hypnotism at first sight. His name was Michael Law, he was an out-of-work documentary film director. We eloped the next day. We went to Wales, to a small cottage on a hill, overlooking Lake Bala.

When we returned to London, where we had nowhere to live, my flat-mates were quite scandalized by my goings-on and voted unanimously to kick me out. I thought them extraordinary, and then I discovered something really odd. I met Jill's boyfriend in the street one day. He was screaming and fulminating with rage and calling her a most cruel bitch. I asked him what the matter was and if he couldn't stand her why did he not move on elsewhere. He said that it was infinitely more awful and terrible. So we went and had a few drinks in the Denmark and he said, 'It's like this, she's been letting me fuck her up her arse for months, but that's it; she's preserving her virginity for her future husband.' It was the most self-righteous hypocritical cant I had ever heard, but it made me laugh rather a lot and I went round to the flat and said to her, 'You are the bottom.'

Michael was much older than me, at least at that time I thought he was. I was nineteen and he was thirty-five. The bearded giant who had introduced us was called Edward. He was a musician and lived with a girl called Zoe, one of Augustus John's daughters. They had taken a lease on a house in Dean Street, which was very pretty, a little Queen Anne house with oak panelling on the corner of St Anne's Court. It had been a brothel before the war. The landlord, who had offices above the Quo Vadis restaurant on the opposite side of the street, wanted to keep his business as clean as possible and let the property on a long lease for a small amount of money. Edward and Zoe restored it with the help of Bill, an architect friend, and because Michael and I were homeless and penniless we moved into the attic. Michael turned to me one day and said your name is Henrietta.

It was 1951 and Soho was alive and kicking, full of people and credit was easy. We led a vagrant life, we never had one single meal at home, two people could lunch at the Gay Hussar for ten bob in those days. Soho was run by a gangster called Billy Hill, and his men were everywhere, collecting protection money from the dutiful and carving up the faces of the obdurate. We were outside the circle of extortion and were left alone, or chatted up: Sid the Swimmer delivered our logs. If you lived in Soho, it was like living in a village, we

25

knew every shopkeeper, every pub and club, Italian, French, Spanish, Polish, Swiss and African. The new Hi-Ho down the alleyway was full of deviant whores, and their protectors, Big Jean and Stout Sally, fought with dustbin lids on Friday evenings. The Lagos Lagoon opposite our drawing-room windows was packed with gambling crazy Africans. I saw a bleeding body with a knife stuck in its back erupt from the club like a clay pigeon one night and thud to the pavement. One day I came home at four in the morning without my latch key and so I was nonplussed. Those lissom black bodies silently formed a pyramid and, taking my hands, ran me up the side of it, on top of their bended backs, to enter through the first floor window, then went on their way laughing.

Our days fell into a pattern. In the morning, latish, we would get up and walk down Dean Street to the Café Torino on the corner of Old Compton Street. It had rose-coloured, marble-tiled tables of antiquity and charm. An Italian mother figure sat behind the minestrone urn. There were vol-au-vents made with chicken and rabbit, steam, warmth and a soft babble of Italian, Spanish, French, Greek, Turkish, German and English voices calling gently to each other. It was a favourite off-duty spot for waiters. Paul, a poet, would be there. We played a game called Analogies.

'What sort of painter are they most like?'

'Ummmm ... sort of Florentine quattrocento, a Medici who holds a buff-coloured doeskin glove in his left hand ...'

'What sort of animal are they like?'

'Oh ... some sort of marsupial, crossed with a deer.'

'I see. Well, what sort of clothes are they like?'

'A grey silk hat.'

'What sort of drink?'

'Dry white wine, Chablis, in the morning, a dry Martini after six, and Armagnac after dinner.'

'Flower?'

'A Madonna lily.'

'It's Michael Law, isn't it?'

'Yes.'

The Café Torino commanded the crossroads and a view of the French Pub opposite. At the appointed time, when the pub had filled up, we would go over, always entering by the left-hand door. Gaston, the landlord, had an exquisite way of lending money. 'Good morning, Gaston, could I have a glass of Pernod – I mean, could you possibly lend me a fiver?' He would return with the drink and hand the change from a fiver back to you with a smile. We would stay till closing time and then go up the road to the wine bar.

Every night we used to go to the Gargoyle. The sun was going down on the Gargoyle, it was like the end of the Café Royal. You took a lift up to the top floor and then walked down a flight of steps into a ballroom, designed by Matisse in the Thirties. The walls and pillars were covered with glass squares which endlessly reflected people, things and events. Here and there the glass had dropped away and the overall picture was one of shattered grandeur, an aged beauty unable to visit the dentist. The band, a bunch of Greek Cypriots named Alexander's Ragtime Band, liked to play the Charleston and the Black Bottom.

The same people went there every night. Cyril Connolly, Angus Wilson, Brian Howard, Simon Asquith, Humphrey Slater, Philip Toynbee, Francis Bacon, Robert Newton, his sister Joy and wife Natalie, Michael Wishart, Lucian Freud, Johnny Minton and twenty sailors, Colquhoun and MacBryde.

It was owned and run by David Tennant – a whim? In the early Fifties everyone was extremely rude to one another. I was terribly shy in this frightening company and couldn't talk at all. Sometimes in the beginning I fell asleep on a little gilt chair. Every night there would be fighting, insults were lobbed into the air. Brian Howard could lob an insulting remark accurately as far as twenty yards, it would transfix and paralyse his victim who had not been aware till too late of the danger. He often made me burst into tears. I started out by being terrified of everybody, a mesmerized rabbit, but I soon got into the spirit and pulled a few beards and hurled some of the faded gilt chairs about. Once Philip Toynbee, who was drinking with Donald Maclean, shot a stream of vomit, like the trumpet of the angel Gabriel, six feet across the room and rolled all over the dance floor, with Donald in his arms, like a battered teddy bear. I was always the youngest person there. I never once walked down the staircase of the Gargoyle without some feelings of dread. Everyone was very critical of one another, but there was a high standard of wit and, provided you were resilient enough, it would act as a stimulus rather than an inhibitor.

Michael was given a job filming aeroplanes near Gosport and I was left alone in Dean Street. I got into a terrible panic. I used to sleep fitfully; things went on all night long in Dean Street. Between two and four o'clock in the morning the clubs would shut and throw their intoxicated custom out on to the street, then the dustmen would do their job, followed by the water cart. As soon as that was finished, the milkman would deliver five thousand bottles of milk to the dairy opposite and after that people would start to get up and racket about. I would lie in bed listening to all this and would start to worry at about nine o'clock in the morning. It got worse and worse and by midday I would be in a lathering sweat of panic, at which point I would make a gigantic effort of will and hurl myself out of bed, into the bath and my clothes, down the stairs and out without time to reflect. I would have avoided the first thing that happened each time I opened our front door had I been able to choose. I found myself in direct confrontation with my reflection in a huge mirror which was part of the frontage of the Quo Vadis opposite. Slamming the door shut behind me, avoiding my still unfamiliar image, eyes lowered, I would spring down the street and from then on it was just like any other day. All I needed was half a crown to buy ten Player's and my first drink, and then I was set for the day, a giddy round of pleasure – bumming, I suppose.

I felt a very strong need to make my own friends, or rather, since they were mostly the same people as Michael's friends, to make friends in my own right.

I went to a party in Montpelier Square with some rather smart but Bohemian people, younger than most of Michael's friends, and I noticed a man sitting on a piano, apparently telling an inexhaustibly funny set of stories, gossip or whatever. People leaned towards him while he gently swung a crossed leg. He was very elegant and I was fascinated and determined to become best friends with him. He was called Francis Wyndham and when we did become friends, which didn't take too long, we used to see each other almost every day, and have lunch in Soho, and go to parties, and whenever we were apart, I would write letters to him because he was the person I needed most in the world and he understood me best. When I got married, he was always my best man and when I had my first child, Joshua, Francis was his godfather. When I went to prison, Francis gave me a little typewriter called Hermes, my ruler. He is the kindest person I know and the most good company. I wish I could have married him. He took me to all sorts of funny things like a pantomime in Balham – *Cinderella*, with Frankie Howerd playing Buttons. He had a passion, for a time, for outings in the suburbs, *Bicycle Thieves* in Tooting. For a while he was the drama critic of the *Queen* and we used to go to all the first nights. In the main these were incredibly boring, things like *The Reluctant Débutante*, and some we could not even sit through. We got a bit of a shock when we saw *Look Back in Anger* and someone mentioned the *Observer*. Nobody had ever heard a modern thing mentioned on the stage before, or seen someone doing their ironing as part of a performance. It came as a bombshell and was the beginning of a whole new movement in the theatre and literature in England. New writers appeared: Colin Wilson, John Osborne, Bernard Kops, Michael Hastings and others. They were called 'angry young men', and to begin with were rather sneered at.

Two other people that I was determined to make friends with because I felt so drawn to them were Lucian Freud and Francis Bacon. They were both young, not particularly well-known painters, but Lucian's hypnotic eyes and Francis's ebullience and charming habit of buying bottles of champagne proved irresistible. I was dancing with Lucian in the Gargoyle one night and said to him, 'I want you.' We made a date to meet at lunchtime the next day in a basement off Brewer Street and there consummated, on the edge of an unwieldy kitchen sink, our friendship.

I fell in love with Lucian and was soon going to his studio in Paddington to be painted every day. It was a romantic work: I was sitting on a bench loosely wrapped in a grey blanket and in the background was the canal with three little ducks swimming along. We used to have oddly timed meals of boiled eggs and toast and watch the contorted figures of meths drinkers creep past the café window.

This went on for over a year and towards the end of it Michael, understandably, got exasperated and went off to Rome to write film scripts in the burgeoning film capital of Europe. Then I missed him. He had told me that if I ever wanted to join him in Rome and get married I was to write to him. I was in Lucian's power, like a mesmerized rabbit, but being in a trance doesn't stop pain and after I discovered someone else's menstrual fluid in what I thought of as my bed I decided that I could take no more and I wrote the letter to Michael.

My aunt Jo was delighted that I was to be married and bought me clothes and linen and towels, all deposited, rather touchingly somehow, in the bottom of a trunk. And so I set out on the voyage.

Chapter Four

My first impression of Rome was disappointing, for the sky was clouded and rain was falling. Michael had a room overlooking the Spanish Steps and opposite the Babington, an English tearoom. We got married, a civil marriage, in the Campidoglio, a beautiful Michelangelo building with a statue of Marcus Aurelius on a horse outside. The mayor, wearing a ribboned sash, officiated. We sat on little gilt chairs in the splashing sunlight; the mayor made a long and entirely incomprehensible speech. Then we were given a luncheon party by Rosie Rodd and Dudley Tooth and caught a train to Naples and Capri for a honeymoon.

We didn't have any money, as usual, but Michael was working on a script for some Italian. One afternoon we went to have some drinks at Gracie Fields' swimming pool. I never had the right sort of clothes, and this time, of course, I didn't have a bathing suit, so I decided to hire one. Reluctantly I climbed into it. It must have dated from the early Thirties: it was black, woollen, down to my knees and full of moth holes.

Emerging from my changing room into the brilliant sunshine of a galaxy of beautiful cosmopolitan butterflies in bikinis, I broke into a run and charged blindly forward into the water wishing I were dead and swam furiously up and down till I was worn out. Feeling better, I looked around me. The pool was empty. Odd, they must all be having lunch, I thought. Perhaps I will too. Swimming to the steps to get out, I realized with a shock that the water level had sunk and the steps were five feet above my head. God, the swimming pool was being emptied and I was stuck in it So I swam round and round like a goldfish. Everyone looked over the edge and screamed with laughter. Bloody wops, I thought. Spaghetti-heads. Michael suddenly noticed my dilemma and rescued me. A rope was thrown to me and, amidst gales of giggles and guffaws, I climbed out. King Farouk was there, surrounded by body-guards. An enormously fat man with a gargantuan appetite and expressionless behind dark glasses. When he jumped into the pool, it more or less emptied, so stout was he. In a night club one evening, called the White Cat, I watched him eat five roast chickens one after the other, when suddenly the lights fused and went up again almost at once. The bodyguards had pulled their guns out and were looking around wildly; the king was on the floor under a tiny table, holding a chicken leg and looking pallid.

Peter Tompkins, an American friend, took us on a pilgrim-age, a beggar's pilgrimage. We drove out of Rome in a jeep. It was a warm night. We drove through a long valley and Peter stopped the jeep. We were captivated, the air was full of the sound of nightingales singing, hundreds of them. We reached a little town at the foot of a mountain. The square was packed with beggars in all stages of decrepitude. At midnight the procession wound off, shuffling, limping, hobbling along. We walked all night up a mountain. At dawn we reached the summit and took our turn to enter a little cave, a shrine. At the end of the cave there was an altar and a charming Victorian painting of three old men with beards sitting on a sofa. The Holy Trinity. Some people had travelled on their knees, so devout were their feelings. We gained plenary absolution – forty years knocked off Purgatory for that pilgrimage. On the way down we encountered several fat friars on donkeys loaded with coffers full of money, from the confessional boxes on high.

We shared a flat with some American scriptwriters who were working on *Attila the Hun*. One of them, Ivan Moffat, was an old friend of Michael's. His father, Curtis Moffat, was a sybarite and Ivan had inherited much of this quality. He called me 'the gentle sloth', which was true enough. We used to go to a night club called the Bear which was by the river in a house that Dante once lived in. The landlady of the flat in via Gregoriana was a descendant of Dante and, in profile, looked exactly like him. She called me the 'lady into fox girl'.

Sometimes I fell into moods of melancholia and depression. I had tried to cut my wrists and failed. The Americans sent me to a recommended Italian psychiatrist, who on my third vis t gave me a dry Martini and made a pass. I repulsed him, shocked by this behaviour in a father figure. *Attila the Hun* was finished and the Roman life ended.

After a year we came back to London and lived in a little flat in Alexandra Terrace. I saw my old friends, lots of painters: Rodrigo Moynihan, Elinor Bellingham-Smith, Robert Buhler, Francis Bacon and, in particular, Johnny Minton.

Johnny lived in a little house in a cul-de-sac at the end of Cheyne Walk called Apollo Place. He liked sailors and one or two were always about, particularly Arnie, a tough innocent from Hull. Johnny looked like a Goya painting; he was quite tall, he had a sort of matchstick body and a very long, thin, dark face with jet-black hair. He was witty and lively and loved dancing. He had quite a lot of money, which he spent rapidly, he liked to have a good time. He worried about his painting, he wasn't sure how good he was or how profound his talent lay.

Arnie became neurotic. One night he said he was sick and tired of everything and was definitely going to end it all and rushed into the kitchen and put his head into the oven. About ten minutes later there was a terrible scream and Arnie rushed out with a sizzling head; it was an electric oven. Puzzled but undeterred, he ran out of the front door, round the corner to the Embankment and vaulted the wall. Into the mud; it was low tide. He was rescued by a delighted crowd from the pub.

Johnny was always looking for a love who would provide a more permanent emotional structure. He met a boy who looked like Michelangelo's David. His name was Norman, an amateur wrestler, body builder and watchmaker. Johnny fell in love with him and Norman went to live in Apollo Place. After some party or other, I found myself with Norman and without a thought we became lovers. This lighthearted affair continued for some time until Johnny found out, and then there was an uproar. Johnny made a fundamental mistake in his strategy when he told Norman that he must choose between him and me, a development that I had not envisaged. Norman vanished. I went to see a film at the Chelsea Classic one

35

afternoon. When I came out of the cinema I went into a telephone box and spoke to Johnny.

'I've just drunk a bottle of gin,' he said, 'and I've been thinking about you.'

I said, 'I'll come and see you then, now.'

We decided to go to Paris but I'd lost my passport, so we got on a train and went to Edinburgh instead. We had an extraordinary week. The weather was amazing, not for nothing is Edinburgh called the Athens of the north. The sky was blue, the sun shone, the snow froze and glittered red and sparkled. We wined and dined and lunched and drank in the pubs for a week. If only we could have made love to each other, we sighed. We took a train to Glasgow and had lunch in Wheeler's on Sauchiehall Street. We rang up Norman, who was at his parents' house, and asked him to join us. We discussed the situation endlessly and went back to London. I was pregnant: Norman decided to choose me. I told Michael, who said he loved me and didn't want me to go anywhere. Norman and I decided to go and see Jeff Bernard, who was living in a little cottage in a field in Suffolk. I rang Michael from Paddington Underground Station. 'Please don't go, not now,' he said. 'I must,' I replied.

Chapter Five

It was unbelievably cold in Jeff's cottage, he had red rashes on his face and the nearest pub was two miles away; I got cystitis. In the end Norman and I decided to live together and we found a bedsitting room in Belsize Park. It was horrible, utterly dispiriting. It was dank and dark and full of linoleum, dark brown paint everywhere, used condoms under the bed, meters for everything – electricity, gas, even water. It smelt of the day and night before yesterday, pale ghosts in dressing-gowns wandered around searching for sixpences and company. Norman went back to work for his father mending watches, and I had ten shillings housekeeping money a day and tried to learn how to cook exquisitely on a single gas ring.

Johnny gave Norman a thousand pounds to buy a house for us to live in. We found one in Upper Street, Islington. It was a very pretty little early Victorian house in which a family of dustmen had lived for a few generations. We scraped it and painted it, and laid carpets and put in a bathroom and rewired it and bought all the furniture from old men in little shops and shacks for about ten pounds: a bentwood rocking chair for two and sixpence, Bristol glass oil-lamps for five shillings, a huge brass bed for thirty bob. I'd never had a home of my own before. I learned how to cook properly and to wash clothes and iron and dust and sweep – actually I became rather fanatical for a bit and overdid things.

Michael divorced me and Norman and I got married in Hampstead register office. It was the middle of a very hot August and I was eight months pregnant. As usual I had no money and nothing to wear and had to put on a tweed winter coat cut in a circle, enormous and totally unsuitable. We had a wedding breakfast in Wheeler's, my favourite restaurant.

I didn't want to have my baby in London, it was such a lovely summer. Norman agreed. We telephoned Edward and Zoe who had left London and lived in Dorset. Their address was White Lackington Mill, Piddletrenthide, Dorchester, Dorset. We explained and they said to come at once and that they were going to France anyway. My son, Joshua, was born on the fourth of October at seven o'clock in the morning. It was a wonderful autumn morning, the sky was blue, the sun shone and I wanted a bottle of champagne. Joshua cried solidly for the first ten days of his life, his face was purple with rage and I very nearly chucked him out of the window. Instead, I loved him.

We came back to London in the late autumn. Islington was cold and grey and windy. I felt very isolated and rather missed my gay life. I never did like north London, even Notting Hill Gate seemed a strange country to me. I loved the river, I always want to be near the river when I'm in London. I am drawn magnetically to it, and most powerfully to the stretch between the end of Chelsea Embankment to Turner's Reach and the King's Arms. Norman worked for his father and in the evening went to acting classes.

Joshua and I were alone for most of the day and some evenings as well. I was both ignorant and neurotic about my baby. I hadn't really ever seen one before. I couldn't bear to be separated from him for one minute. I thought that when I wasn't with him he would stop breathing, so I carried him about with me, from room to room in his blue wicker Moses basket. Sometimes I would have a lunch party on Sunday afternoon. Johnny would come and so would Colin MacInnes. Johnny loved Joshua. He used to laugh at him and make Joshua giggle and wonder what Joshua's first words would be.

A year passed and we went back to Piddletrenthide for the summer. Norman got a job pushing out boats on Weymouth Sands. Sometimes we went to Chesil Bank to swim and one hot, shimmering August afternoon I had the pleasure to see, as if it were a mirage, a collection of black-skirted and veiled nuns playing beach cricket with an impressive black bishop in his purple vest and gaiters, a grinning face with white, white teeth.

My best girlfriend, Caryl Chance, returned with two children from Canada, where she had been for two years, and came to stay with us. When we were younger, we had had many good times together, dressing up in black satin dresses and white fox furs and disporting ourselves in expensive restaurants like the Mirabelle and the 21 Room and going on to night clubs like Les Ambassadeurs, the Milroy and Churchill's. Caryl always had somebody on to whom she could offload the bill, and I provided the necessary wild wilfulness and energy for the initial impetus of entry. I loved Caryl, she never bored me. One night, sitting in the seductive gloom of

Churchill's, I pulled out a Havana cigar, which I was in the habit of smoking at that time. A waiter appeared and with a flourish lit it. He did not disappear, as he should have done, but stood about in front of our table giggling and lighting more matches for me. Puzzled, I examined my cigar and realized with a sudden jolt that I was smoking a super Tampax, selected at random from the dubious contents of my bag. Caryl and I had a friend, a young man called Tony Hubbard, our steamer. He was very rich and spoilt and extravagant, generous and musically gifted. He entertained us to endless lunches, visits to Muriel's, dinners, night clubs and a visit to Paris, to celebrate the 'quatorze juillet' in a specially chartered Dove.

I became pregnant again. We left Dorset and Caryl and her children came back to London with us to live in Islington. Caryl got a job and I got a job and we hired a nanny, a deeply suspicious, cleft-palated, scrawny blonde girl with a crew cut, called Jean. Irish and somewhat of a slut, she was kind-hearted, easy-going, inefficient and fond of children.

My job was irresistibly appealing to me. It was to run the coffee bar of David Archer's new bookshop in Greek Street, Soho, opposite the stage door of the Palace Theatre. David Archer and his friend John Deakin were old friends of mine. I had spent my early youth drinking in the same places as they did and this bond, once forged, is impossible to overlook. Archer was a man the like of whom will not be seen again: gently born, eccentrically orientated, altruistically minded, hysterically tempered, kind, perceptive, a left-wing Fascist and patron saint of the Forties and Fifties poets. A sort of Fred Winter of the literary world with a fastidious nose and a total lack of interest in anything that was less than first rate. He had first published Dylan Thomas, George Barker, David Gascoyne, Sidney Graham and the very first novel by Graham Greene. His publishing house was called the Parton Press and it was entirely financed by David. He was so generous-minded that he let his authors own their own copyright. Of course he never managed to recoup any money. As soon as his authors became successful, which they invariably did, they would transfer to a bigger house with greater powers of distribution.

The manager of the bookshop was a man called Ralph Abercrombie, the son of the poet Lascelles Abercrombie; he had been the manager of David's first bookshop in Red Lion Square. His speciality was second-hand books.

John Deakin, who was a talented photographer, took a photograph of me, blew it up to nine feet by seven and stuck it in the alcove at the back of the shop, which became my coffee bar. We bought a coffee machine, some cups and saucers, a drying-up cloth or two and opened. I used to buy brown and white rolls from Floris and pâté and cheese and watercress and hard-boiled eggs and sell them at absurdly low prices, making a point of giving away food that hadn't been sold the day before to those who had no money.

David wasn't the slightest bit interested in selling any books, he just liked to be surrounded by them. Passing strangers would wander in and ask for a copy of *The Outsider*, which was selling like hot cakes at that time. We had about sixty copies stuck away on a back shelf somewhere. David would become very flustered and say, 'No, no, no, we haven't anything like that here. You'd do much better to go up the street to Charing Cross Road to Foyle's. Good morning.' This exchange would elicit screams of rage from Ralph, Deakin and me. Of course what David wanted was a literary salon in the style of Madame de Staël, and he got it. Colin Wilson, Christopher Logue, Colin MacInnes, Michael Hastings, George Barker and many others came in every day, drank endless cups of coffee and talked voraciously, but never bought a book.

David had a charming but infuriating habit of raiding the till as drink and lunchtime became a pressing need. He would start rattling out staccato sentences about this and that and look wildly about him, then his right hand would furtively make its way into the till, remove a bunch of pound notes and stuff them triumphantly into his pocket. He would stand up and announce his departure to the Coach and Horses up the road and ask us to join him 'in a second'.

His sweetness was such that if he met one of the many itinerant writers he knew, he would stuff a fiver in a matchbox which he would contrive for the young man to end up with, a wonderful surprise when he lit up a Woodbine. Ralph and I decided this wouldn't do, so we bought a cash box with a key, which David wasn't allowed to keep. One night I had been drinking somewhere or other and went back to the shop to fetch something that I had left behind. All the lights were on, and there was David, purple in the face and sweating, jumping furiously up and down on the cash box in a vain attempt to burst it open. He looked up. 'Silly old me,' he said sadly.

Ralph had arranged a deal to supply American universities with books from his second-hand list, financially a sound idea. One day we went down into the cellar for something and found enormous crates and tea chests, full of books, parcelled up and even addressed to their destination, but somehow forgotten about and never posted; I don't believe they ever were, either.

With my favourite bunny in Simla

Dreaming in a friend's garden

Michael and me on the Capitoline Hill on our wedding day

A Deakin photograph, missing only the hypodermic syringe in the painting

A Bacon portrait from a Deakin photograph showing how closely the artist
worked from the photographic medium

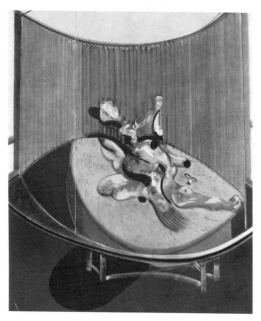

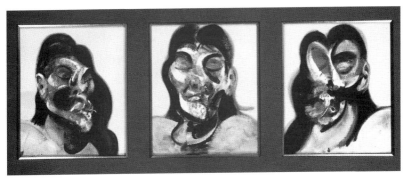

A very gypsy looking triptych of me in the Sixties

Dom Moraes, the poet, having won the Hawthornden prize

Norman Bowler in the Fifties on show on the beach

Pensive in the late Fifties in my studio in Chelsea

Me outside my favourite place, the French Pub, in the late Fifties

Johnny Minton – looking his most adorable and suave best

My beloved children, Joshua and Caroline, in my studio. A Deakin photograph, the only one of children that I know of

A more informal Deakin photograph

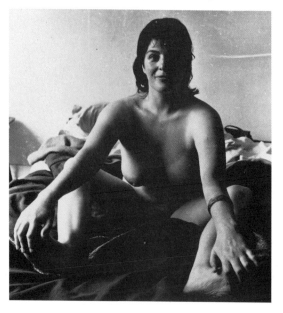

An idyllic holiday on the barge *Greylag* – the first two weeks in June in the late Sixties

On the road with Mark Palmer and John Michell. My hippy life at its most beguiling.
About 1973

Below, left: Mark, leading a 'for sale' string of horses at the gypsy fair, Appleby.
He is followed by two lurchers
Below, right: Lucian riding a coloured mare with two foals at the Grove in the Seventies

Deakin provided a sensation one morning. He went into the Golden Lion at opening time, as was his wont, and asked for his usual, a large glass of white wine, which he drained to the dregs in one enormous gulp. He fell to the floor unconscious. Panic and consternation. What had happened? A new barman had served him with a large glass of Parozone, which he had not realized was always kept on the bar in a white wine bottle. A lesser man would have died at once. Not Deakin. He was flown to Charing Cross Hospital, stomach-pumped and emerged later in the day, chirpy as ever and demanding drinks.

One afternoon David and I were having a drink in the Colony Room. 'Hello, cunty,' Muriel, the owner, greeted me as usual. We sat down on a banquette and David pulled some crumpled sheets of typescript from his pocket. 'I wish you'd read these poems,' he said, 'they're by a young Indian boy called Dom Moraes. I might want to publish them. What do you think?' I said I liked them and he seemed relieved and pleased and stuffed them back in his pocket. A few days later a slender, fawn-eyed boy wandered into the shop. Dom. He had long eloquent hands, smoked continuously and remained totally silent. He came every day, stayed all day and finally arrived so early in the morning that he was able to help me do the shopping. One day he uttered his first words to me. 'Would you care to have lunch with me?'

'Yes,' I said, astounded, 'I would, thank you.'

We ate and drank in complete silence at the bar in Wheeler's. I could think of nothing to say and neither could he, but I became aware of the strongest emotional vibrations and tensions coming from him. It continued thus for some time, though we progressed enough to exchange pleasantries.

Norman became like an outraged bull and beat me up one night when I came home late. 'But I haven't done anything,' I screamed, bewildered. 'He's just my friend.'

The bookshop had been open for three months, I was six months pregnant and was in the Coach and Horses having a lunchtime drink, when the air around me went heavy and I fainted. I took no especial notice, I thought it was just something that happened if one was pregnant and perhaps overtired. The next day the same thing happened and that night I woke up feeling deathly cold and shivering uncontrollably. 'Help me to have a hot bath,' I chattered to Norman, 'I feel as if I'm dying.' It occurred to me to take my temperature. It was 101 degrees, I was rather frightened. My doctor arrived and said that he didn't know what it was but that it looked like pylitis, a kidney trouble. He called an ambulance and I was whisked away to the Whittington Hospital in Highgate. Here things became very strange indeed. It was the year of the Hungarian revolution and the last thing I remember hearing when I left home was a broadcast from Radio Free Hungary imploring the world for help. A voice was saying, 'Somebody must come to our aid, the Russians are here, I can hear the sound of tanks . . . Somebody come.' The radio went silent. It was too late.

I was put into a ward full of pregnant ladies with various gynaecological ailments, all quite merry and cosy. My temperature rose and fell with the rapidity of a yo-yo, from 104 down to 96 and back again. I felt as if I was either being burnt at the stake or underneath the polar ice-cap. I got the most awful diarrhoea, so I sat on a bedpan all day and most of the night long. I was given no treatment because the doctors could not diagnose what was the matter with me. I became worse and was convinced that someone had set fire to my bed. I became a squadron leader at the head of a flight of bombers whose mission it was to bomb the Russian tanks which had invaded Hungary. To keep up my spirits I sang hymns, the Old Hundredth, all night long. I was very, very unpopular in that ward.

One morning my bed was surrounded by puzzled doctors. The staff nurse pulled up my nightdress over my distended stomach. There was a loud gasp of consternation and amazement from the company. I looked down and saw, as if it were a flower garden, scores of little red roses dotted all over my stomach. 'Typhoid,' they said. 'Oh Christ. We must get rid of her, now, at once. Ring up the fever ward of the Royal Free Hospital and tell them to get a bed ready.'

I was wheeled on a trolley along endless, grey, draughty passages until we stopped at the entrance of Ward 10 and in we went. People came up to me and said, 'Hello.'

'Don't come near me, I've got typhoid fever,' I croaked.

Another panic, this time amongst the patients, who all said they wanted to leave, then and there. Sister was furious but I was only trying to be helpful. I was installed in a glass box at the end of the ward opposite Sister's office. Various antibiotics were prescribed and I began to come down from my high fever; horrible, much nastier than being very ill. The morning round of doctors, nurses and students arrived.

'Put out your tongue, Mrs Bowler,' they commanded.

I protruded the disgusting, withered little black and green stick that my tongue had become, as far as it would go.

'Just look at that,' the consultant mused. 'Ten years ago she

45

would have been dead by now. As it is, she'll probably miscarry.'

'Like hell, I will,' I swore to myself.

It was a bizarre situation that I was in. Ward 10 was an abortion ward – that is, abortions were not performed in it but the near dying, fevered, bleeding bodies of women who had stuck knitting needles up themselves were brought in and resuscitated. I, for once, was white lamb instead of black sheep. My bed was next to the operating theatre and surgeons would wave at me round the corner, their boots and white coats spotted with blood.

I was in hospital a long time, about three months. It was an unhappy place. At night cries and sobs rent the air – women who were having a lonely, miserable and painful time. Ruddy, the ward sister, was a Catholic: no advice was ever given to patients about methods of contraception. One girl, whom I recognized from the old days in St Anne's Alley, had been in four times already that year. She was a coloured girl. The staff treated her like dirt. 'Not you again,' they rasped at her. 'We shouldn't really let you into this ward, but you look as if you are dying, so I suppose we'll have to. Just on the grounds of humanitarianism, you understand.' The poor wretched girl turned her face to the wall and suffered alone.

Christmas Eve came round. Just as we had all got to sleep, the ward filled with cloaked nurses carrying lamps and exhorting us to wassail, rejoice and be generally grateful that our saviour had been born this day. In the morning we were given a glass of sherry and a Guinness. Several doctors – surgeons, I believe – came in, dressed as high-class chefs, brandishing carving knives and forks, and proceeded to carve four turkeys in record time. I thought how gruesome, what a dire black joke, for they were the same men who had scraped clean the wombs of most of the ladies in that ward. A Turkish lady was brought in. Every night she would sidle out of the ward, and every night she was brought back by the night porter on duty at the gate, slung over his shoulder and sobbing uncontrollably. In the end the Turkish consul was summoned and it transpired that her man had left her, taking all her clothes and furniture and money. It was a rule in the hospital that a patient was not allowed to leave in a nightdress, so her dilemma was grave.

A physiotherapist came to visit me every afternoon to exercise all my unused muscles. I told her that I was really very frightened of having a baby because it had been something of an ordeal when Joshua was born. She said, 'You silly thing, I'll teach you to relax.' And so she did. Every day, when we had finished the heave-hoing and strengthening-the-legs stuff, she would make me lie on my side and shut my eyes while she spoke to me. 'Imagine you are lying in space on a black velvet cloud, you're sinking deeper into it, you can't feel the weight of your body, deeper and deeper you sink . . .' At which point I generally fell asleep and when I woke up I felt newly born, so fresh was I.

The day came for me to walk again, I'd been three months in bed. 'Take it easy,' they said. 'Go slowly,' they advised. 'You'll find it quite hard to keep your balance, let alone take a few steps.' I jumped out of bed, took two tiny, tottering steps and collapsed in a huge jelly-like heap on the floor, incapacitated and furious. Ward 10 and its attendant staff lolled about screaming with laughter. I was shown how to weave and I chose to make a lampshade. The lengths of cane which I was working with always found a way of tripping up anyone passing my bed. I was moved into a little side room. I had become a carrier, which meant that I was not in an active stage of the disease but the germ was thriving away happily in the gall bladder and so could be transmitted to others.

My friends were kind and loyal and visited me every night, which, after all, since most of them would have preferred to spend the time in a pub, was a pretty noble gesture. Dom came every day, silent as ever but bearing gifts of Gitanes, grapes and books of George Barker's poetry. One afternoon Norman arrived and sat down on the edge of my bed and said, 'Something terrible has happened.'

I screamed, 'Joshua's dead.'

'No,' Norman answered. 'Johnny is dead. They think that he killed himself and he's left you his house in Chelsea. It's in his will.' The brightness of the afternoon sunlight in the little room faded away and I thought I was dying too. I was drawn down an apparently endless tunnel with no light at either end. Oh Johnny, how I love you, and now all I have is to think of you every single day of my life, and it will take a long time for the pain and regret to metamorphosize into the golden butterfly which is your soul.

The next day, suddenly, miraculously, Sister Ruddy came into my room and said, 'All's well, my dear. The typhoid germs have disappeared from your body. Odd, really, isn't it?'

'No, not really,' I said, 'I've been praying for that to happen.'

So I was moved to the main building, just for safety's sake. They were very kind to me, as indeed everyone in the fever hospital had been. I was allowed to go out in the afternoons, but had to be back six hours earlier than Cinderella. I spent an afternoon with Elinor and Rodrigo Moynihan and their son John and some other people, and I felt this little nagging pain in my back and thought, To hell with it. It was so mild. Suddenly at curfew time, six o'clock, I realized that these little niggling pains were labour pains and I'd better beat it back to Liverpool Road – in fact, zap back.

I lay in bed in the labour ward remembering what my physiotherapist had taught me and I sank back into the old black velvet cloud. They gave me a shot of pethidine, usually used on sick sheep, I'm told. I made up three poems, sang seven songs and sat up to watch my baby daughter enter our world. All went very well. 'My word,' shouted the Pakistani doctor, 'what a lucky girl you are.' But I blessed my physiotherapist.

A fortnight later I was allowed to go home, which was, after all, just down the road. I was petrified with fear, the traffic was trying to kill me. I was reunited with my son, Joshua, superficially a golden-haired cherub but with a will of steel.

My old friend Caryl Chance and her two children came to stay with us in Islington. We had this ridiculous nanny person and Caryl had a job in the beauty department of Selfridges. One morning she came into my bedroom, where Norman and I were peacefully surfacing from the blackness of night. 'I'm late,' she said. 'Would you kindly give me a lift to work?'

He screamed at her, 'Piss off, you fucking old cow, can't you leave me in peace?'

I sat bolt upright in bed and said, 'You've been having an affair with Caryl all this time. She's my best friend and I've been almost dying in hospital and having your blasted baby and all the time you've been screwing her all over London and you never even told me or warned me about it.'

I was absolutely certain of this, I knew that Norman would

49

never have spoken to her in that vein unless he had formed some sort of really intimate relationship with her. He didn't bother to deny it at all and said that it was all true but what did I expect him to do since I had been, as he put it, out of action for over three months. He got up and went off to work.

In a rather dazed state I packed my things, ordered a pantechnicon, wrapped up the babies, asked nanny if she wanted to come or stay behind, informed Caryl that I felt I had to leave.

She said, 'Oh, please let me come with you.'

'Not on your nelly,' I wept furiously at her.

Chapter Six

Then I left Islington for ever and came to my new home in Chelsea, to the house that Johnny had the wisdom to give to me, number 9 Apollo Place, Cheyne Walk. It was in a little cul-de-sac behind the King's Arms. It was like an Arabic house, with a little doorway, bare wall, railings and nothing else to be seen. But inside it was a lovely surprise. Long passages, high ceilings, a large kitchen and bathroom. Upstairs was even nicer. A flight of red-carpeted stairs led to a vast studio with rafters and beams. There was an enormous fireplace at the far end of the room. Three large windows looked out on to the walled garden, which was paved with large stones and studded with enormous jars full of azaleas, magnolias, roses, lilies of the valley and bay trees. One of the walls was covered with wisteria and the garden was always full of birds, singing and nesting.

It was the most peaceful place. For some odd acoustic reason no sound of traffic could be heard from Cheyne Walk, which was, after all, just round the corner; only the sound of tugs and barges on the river filtered through. I knew at once that my children and I would be very happy in that house.

Penniless, as usual, I sought a job at the Alfred Marks Bureau and was referred to a man named Miller who sold anti-smoking pills – Nico-Brevin was the trade name for this firm. My job was dull, mostly typing out invoices, and I sat in an office overlooking Golden Square, chain-smoking and writing letters which told people that most likely the odds were that the next Woodbine or whatever they smoked would be their last . . . unless they turned to Nico-Brevin for salvation. My boss, the patent owner of this stuff, also smoked like a chimney, but on the plus side, he adored the pair of herons that nested each year on an island in St James's Park, visited them daily with goodies and nearly died with grief one year when they were seen no more.

Dom and I became lovers in a little Asiatic boarding house somewhere in Kensington which his father had installed him in, to keep him safe before he went up to Oxford. We became lovers and remained lovers for ten years.

I met a friend of mine called Geoffrey Rigby in the French Pub one day. I'd just had all my hair cut off and curled and dyed red and looked rather smart. He said, 'Would you like to come and be my assistant? I've got a job as the television director in an advertising agency.'

'Yes, yes,' I shouted. 'I've just been sacked from the smoking set-up because of my dilatory attendance. The only thing is I don't know one single thing about advertising and I've never seen a television-set in my life.'

'It doesn't matter,' he replied. 'You were married to Michael, weren't you, and you've knocked about Rome with a few film people? Write up a little history of yourself, use your imagination a bit, you know. Come to Brook Street at eleven o'clock tomorrow morning. For God's sake, look good and let me do the talking.' It was a cinch. I was in.

I made bloomer after bloomer – asked a television cameraman where he kept the film, that sort of thing – but Geoffrey protected me and taught me everything I needed to know and how to avoid revealing my ignorance about the things that I didn't know by talking very fast about something close but different. The first important thing was to make firm friends with the agency's clients who used television advertising. This was done by making friends with the agency's accountant and getting fixed up with an expense account. Then nice long luncheons at all my favourite restaurants, followed by hard work on the scripts the clients wanted. More hard work with our film and TV directors liaising closely on the set so that my product – pens, frozen foods, tobacco, cars and so on – would always get an extra long close-up. The clients would be delighted, writing to the agency to say how well they thought their product had been shown on the box, and I would get a pat on the back from the creative director, who knew only about painting and poems, and my salary went up and my expense account expanded and I took taxis everywhere and rather enjoyed the whole thing.

Things at home were less satisfactory. I had to depend on my cleft-palated nanny, Jean, to look after the children, who were only tiny, to cook, shop, wash and clean, and it wasn't working. She wasn't capable and she was wearing all my clothes and drinking my drink and, I suspected, having her boyfriends round in the afternoon instead of taking the children to Battersea Park. So I told her to put an ad in the paper shop and find someone to do the cleaning. Soon after this I noticed a miraculous change. The floors were shining and polished, everything gleamed, the children looked wonderful, sheets and even nappies were ironed. Order prevailed. I asked Jean who she had found to help her like this. She pointed at the buildings opposite and said, 'Oh, a little old Irish lady who lives with her daughter, number 11, I think. She's called Mary Grice.' I rushed over, tore up the stairs and knocked on the door. It was opened by a tiny, delicate, sad-faced, faery-like creature who gave me a huge, toothless grin.

'You're wonderful,' I said. 'I love you. I want you to come and live with me for ever. You're the only person in the world, please come.' I hugged her and felt so safe.

'Ah,' she said, 'you're just like one of me own daughters, Hennyietta. But I couldn't do anyone out of a job.'

'Well, if Jean goes, will you come then?'

'Yes,' she said, 'I'll do that and I'll still be near me own.' Jean went and Nana came and it was like heaven.

Looking back on that particular period of my life – it lasted eight or nine years – I think it was the happiest and most productive time I have ever experienced. I was independent in my own house, with my children and with Nan who was a combination of friend, mother and guardian angel with a taste for whisky. Totally reliable she was, and totally loving and careful. When I followed her advice, all went well; when I ignored it, she was always proved right and I wrong. That is to say, what she advised was always to my advantage. She had oracular gifts, which, when not obeyed, moved me from the white square on to the black. Her appraisal of my friends was infallible: if she didn't like them, they were wrong for me. She did like most of them and they loved her; they came to the house as much to see her as they did me. She loved young

54

men, going to the pub round the corner and dancing. Her favourite tune was Bill Haley's 'Rock Around the Clock', and we did.

Dom was her favourite and she called him Dommy. David Archer's bookshop had inevitably gone bankrupt, but he had published Dom's first book of poems, *A Beginning,* and it won the Hawthornden Prize, which hadn't been awarded for fourteen years. We had lunch at the Ritz with Lord David Cecil and L. P. Hartley, who were two of the judges and trustees of the prize. Lord David told a ridiculous joke about Mrs Siddons and the Duke of Buckingham, two species of roses, being found together in the same bed in the Vicar of Bray's garden. Mr Hartley pinched Dom's thighs and bottom and we proceeded to a merry prize-giving, £100 and a party at Apollo afterwards. I remember Stephen Spender displaying his beautiful profile to great advantage against the white walls and Nan performing a spirited Black Bottom with David Archer, John Deakin tipsily photographing everything with aplomb and accuracy.

Dom was up at Oxford for three years and I used to visit him as often as I could and vice versa. He had a lot of friends, Peter Levi, SJ, who had not then been ordained, Del Kolve, an American, John Fuller, Roy Fuller's son, Patrick Garland and some joke versions of standard Oxford types. We did some lovely things: punting on the Isis on hot sparkling June afternoons, swigging champagne and swallowing strawberries and cream accompanied by beauties in white flannels and straw hats. Dinner parties, sherry parties, walks through Christ Church Meadows in the early-morning dew, picnics and swimming parties. Dom's rooms had once been occupied by T. E. Lawrence and the stone embrasure in the window had been worn thin by the countless pairs of knees of those looking out at the view, which was of a gentlemen's lavatory. We gave one sherry party in honour of, and in order to pacify, the Master of Jesus, a Mr Christie. I filled the room with white flowers and hoped for the best. I was always too late in leaving Dom's rooms and either had to stay the night, which was tricky in the morning when his scout came to wake him up, or to climb over the college wall, which was dangerous because of the spikes on it. The moral tutor was always on the prowl at this time of night and we once had to hide in two dustbins while he nosed about, like Beckett's people in *Fin de Partie*. I often took a room at the Turl, which provided a Gideon Bible, and there I partially and drunkenly attempted to assimilate St John the Divine's revelations.

At Eastertime Dom and I went to Paris. Lovely. I knew all the bits and pieces of Paris quite well from my teen days, so I was quite happy to sit in the sun outside the Deux Magots and drink Pernod. One midday we were doing just this and into our line of vision walked two weird-looking folk. One was gangly and ungainly with a massively intelligent face and forehead, he looked like a Jew. The other was small, goatlike, – kidlike, actually – masses of black curls, the face of a fallen angel, an Italian cherub with a Greek godfather and Caravaggio did the rest. They were proceeding with much animation and apparently no particular direction in mind. However, like a game of snakes and ladders, they suddenly zoomed straight up to our saucer-laden table.

'Hi, man . . . You're Dom Moraes. We are Ginsberg and Corso.'

'How do you do?' Dom answered, looking pleased.

I said, 'Hello, shall we all have another drink?' Pernod, of course.

Later they said, 'Come to breakfast, we're into Japanese Zen. Bill will be there, Burroughs.'

We walked around some corners, everything becoming narrower and more and more confusing. We came to rue Git le Coeur, turned into a pretty villainous Algerian hotel, walked up the stairs and went into a small, airless, smoky room. A sombre, grey figure was sitting on a bed.

'Good day,' he said. 'I hate women. Women are like birds, they sit on the window-sill and tap, tap, tap on the glass. Come here' – he beckoned me to sit on the bed beside him – 'I'll show you something. These are my tracks.' He carefully rolled up his grey trouser legs to above his knees. I looked at the network of scar tissue, which outlined every vein. Scar tissue, dead cells, just a memory.

Gregory Corso shoved a large, rather clumsy cigarette into my hand. 'Get high.'

I smoked some of it and went off to find the lavatory. It was tiny and the hole in the middle was blocked by the most enormous turd in the world. The stench of ammonia killed the oxygen supply and as I peed over the turd, tears poured out of my eyes and down my face, cascading on to my collarbones. I stumbled back.

'It's nothing to do with any of you,' I said aggressively, defensively and passionately.

'No, it's the Turk downstairs. Same thing every morning.'

They said that they intended to come to London, reckoning it, by and large, to be the birthplace of poetry.

When they arrived, Ginsberg gave a poetry reading at the

ICI, which luckily has a bar. He read his long poem *Howl*: 'I saw the best minds of my generation destroyed . . .'

I sat in my seat and shivered, it is a prophetic poem. He read it well, the temperature in the room dropped to a bitter cold.

Afterwards we went to the nearest pub to warm up. Allen and Gregory had a drink or two and started to undress, screaming passionately, 'You bloody English mother-fuckers. You kill your poets. All the greatest, you murder them. Keats, Shelley, Byron, John Clare.'

They removed their trousers and we were shown out of the house and warned to never ever show our faces again. Dom suggested that they should go to Oxford to do a reading at the New College poetry society and to meet W. H. Auden who had the chair of poetry at that time. They went. Gregory read some of his poems to the New College lot. One poem was in praise of the hydrogen bomb. Because of the prevailing preponderance of left-wingers in this group, the emotional atmosphere rose sharply and before long Gregory was sitting in the middle of a circle of infuriated intellectuals, who took off their shoes and bombarded him unmercifully with them. Gregory continued to read imperturbably until the end. Then he looked around him and said, 'Hey, I thought you cats didn't dig violence.'

They rushed into the Kardomah Café, in which place W. H. Auden could be found about eleven o'clock each day, prostrated themselves on the floor and kissed the old carpet slippers that were part of his morning garb. They went on a tour of Christ Church chapel and threw cannabis seeds like confetti wherever they went. The first transatlantic beatniks had arrived.

Chapter Seven

Dom and I were married in the Chelsea register office in 1961. Years later, when I went to get a copy of the marriage certificate, it was found not to exist and I doubted the validity of the ceremony altogether. A little old dusty lady suddenly said, 'I remember you, you came out of the Eight Bells opposite. You were wearing white gloves and you waved to me.' She produced a cobwebbed file and waved it triumphantly.

We honeymooned. We caught the Orient-Simplon Express from Paris to Athens. We had a first-class Pullman compartment, Victorian mahogany and polished brass fittings, pink silk shaded lamps, a drawing-room which miraculously changed into a crisp, snowy-sheeted bedroom at night. It took four days to reach Athens, and although the restaurant car disappeared somewhere in Yugoslavia for a time, there is no better way to travel. It was late March, and Athens was cold, snowing and flowerless. We met Suna Portman, an old friend, and Gregory Corso.

'Hello, man, I've never been on a honeymoon before.'

We decided on a Peloponnesian journey and hired a Fiat, which proved to be not quite large enough. It was a miraculous time, the country was deserted and as we progressed the twentieth century faded away. Corinth seemed still to be a brash, moneyed sea port, Epidaurus a healing centre, Delphi a blaze of light on the hillside looking over the silver-blue olive groves to the sea. En route, Gregory befriended a donkey and fed it three quarters of a bottle of Greek brandy. It galloped drunkenly after the car, trumpeting and braying like some herald of a troupe of clowns. In Arakhova, a Turkish village built on the edge of a cliff, I looked through the cracks in my bedroom floor and saw the valley a thousand feet below. We were suspended in space, resting on a couple of old struts. The next morning we had to rescue Gregory from the police station, where he had been taken for exhibiting indecent and insulting behaviour to all and sundry. The Greeks dislike undignified conduct from foreigners.

We arrived in Mycenae in the late afternoon. The sky was full of dark, lowering purple clouds, the wind moaned, snowflakes hit the eyeballs with venom. We drove to the inn La Belle Hélène. The owner's name was Agamemnon. As we signed the register, I flipped back a few pages and found a page full of the signatures of the inner circle of the Third Reich, 'Hermann Goering' in small and dainty writing. Schliemann, the archaeologist who excavated Mycenae, must have been a feather in the cap of the German occultists in their ceaseless quest for mythological identification. We walked past Clytemnestra's beehive-shaped tomb and towards the towering stone lion gateway. Gregory, howling and roaring, jumped down from the top. We stared into the bramble-obscured, dark, gaping hole, down which Orestes fled from the Furies having killed his mother's lover. I saw dark rivulets of blood congealing in the stone causeways and felt the impact of a darkly ominous drama. The next morning, when we woke up, the sky was pale blue and cloudless and the stark hillside was covered in windflowers, like jewels thrown from the careless hand of a giant.

From Athens we flew to Tel Aviv. Dom had a commission to cover the Eichmann trial for *The Times* of India. I wandered through an orange grove, smelling for the first time the heavenly scent of the blossom. Israel was in a state of extreme tension and nervous irritability. We were given a press car with a driver called Nissim, which means 'miracle', and travelled from the pastoral lands and lakes of Galilee down to the desert tip of the Negev and the port of Eilat, where Solomon received the Queen of Sheba.

The trial was to be held in Jerusalem. The courtroom was a newly built theatre, Beit Haam, 'house of the people'. Eichmann was placed in a bullet-proof glass box on the stage, like a Francis Bacon painting of a pope. He sat at an oak table piled high with his papers, wearing an old pair of carpet slippers. The judges and jury sat in the orchestra pit and the witnesses climbed a circular staircase to the edge of the stage. The first three days were spent establishing the legal precedent for a sovereign state to kidnap a prisoner. The charge was genocide. Witness after witness was called and gave their horrifying testimony. I saw a row of hardened French journalists in tears. There were outcries from the public gallery. Eichmann was impassive. He denied every charge, denied his identification by witnesses in court, denied his signature on documents authorizing the final extermination plans, denied kicking a boy to death for stealing a peach, admitted only to obeying orders from above. He was obdurate and only once did he react as a human being. The lights fused one morning for a few seconds and when they went up he was crouching, cowering under the oak table, his slippers kicked off in haste. He was obviously guilty.

We came back to England on a cargo ship, which carried Israeli cans of tomato juice and melons. It was a three-week voyage but took longer as we quite often broke down and drifted off course. There were thirteen passengers, very oddly assorted and somewhat unstable. The officers were all Scots and at each other's throats. Meals, which we all took at the captain's table, were subject to violent outbreaks between the chief engineer and the first mate, threats of suicide from a lady from Golders Green and fits of irrepressible giggles from the rest of us.

Chapter Eight

Misunderstandings arose. I became disorientated. I could not understand Dom's need to tell lies, or at best to evade the truth. If, for instance, I asked him how he had returned home after an absence, he would reply that he had travelled homeward on a number 19 bus. By chance, as it were, the fact that he'd come home on a number 22, or by taxi, would emerge. Perhaps I did not understand that his motives were to produce reasons for events that he imagined would please me, rather than tell the truth, however banal, shocking or amazing. I was much too neurotic for his delicate nervous system, and we both drank too much.

One evening, we went to the Odeon, Marble Arch, to see an Elvis Presley movie called *Jailhouse Rock*. It was 1963. Usually I liked to sit in the front circle seats, but that night, when we got to the box office, I insisted that we should sit in the back stalls. Halfway through the film, just as Elvis performs the jailhouse rock, there was a loud and terrifying explosion.

Rumbles and more smaller explosions followed, the air filled with dust. Whirling pieces of severed film appeared on the screen. I thought that someone had put a bomb in the projection box. The cinema was full of screams. The audience crowded the exits, although the house lights were still down. I remembered reading somewhere that the only possible thing to do in such a situation was to sit tight, work out exactly what was happening and act later. Pictures of being trampled to death flew through my brain.

'We must not move yet.'

I said this in such an authoritative tone, that we did nothing but sit still and wait for the panic to subside. Finally, when it became obvious that there was no fire, we exited and made for the front foyer. People round us were reeling about the place, wounded and bleeding. Ambulances arrived, the stretcher men got to work. Chaos was rampant.

'What the hell happened?'

'The central chandelier suddenly broke out of its moorings and fell into the middle of the front circle,' someone hissed. 'There are lots of dead ones about.'

'How much did it weigh?'

'A couple of tons.'

We went off to drink brandy. It warms the cockles of the heart.

One day Dom didn't come home. Nan and I started to worry, so we got into a taxi and went off on a Dom hunt. In the end, after a lot of red herrings and false trails we ran him to earth in an extraordinary tenement in Pimlico. He was in a frightful condition. Shaking, trembling, he looked ill and in need of care and attention. We ignored all protests and dragged him off, helped him into the taxi and went home, where we found, to our dismay, that his thick black hair was lousy, hundreds of tiny white eggs showed up clearly.

One fine morning Dom said, 'Look, darling, I'm off to the pub, just going to get some cigarettes. See you in about ten minutes.' He didn't come back and I couldn't find him anywhere. For the next few months I heard his voice everywhere, I heard him talking to Nanny in the kitchen, I heard his footfall on the studio stairs and the sound of him crossing the room but he was never there. I passed through all the stages of desolation through to anger and madness. Dom had vanished, completely. He closed the front door behind him and disappeared. I wept on Nana's tiny chest.

'He's gone for ever, Nan, I know it, yes.'

'Ah, sure, Hennyietta, he'll be back, sure he will.'

'No, no, no.'

Eighteen months later, Hussein and I were sitting in the Gilded Cage on the King's Road. After a bit I said, 'Look, Hussein, it's all a bit weird, but three people have walked past us in the last twenty minutes and all of them look very like Dom and I haven't seen him for nearly two years.' Precisely on cue, Dom walked by, crossed the road and went into a house in Wellington Square. 'Let's go,' I said. We rang the doorbell and Shura, the most hospitable man in the world, opened his front door. He seemed a bit nervous but he had to let us in, it was too foreign to his nature not to. Through the hall, upstairs in the drawing-room, sat the delinquent Dom, startled by our appearance. He was sitting in front of a wood fire and sipping, or rather swallowing, tumblers of Russian vodka. Shura panted into the room.

'It's odd. They say, or rather they presume, that because I

have a lot of the real thing, I'm a Russian spy, and they won't give me a British passport. I never keep any caviare, I can't afford it. They never take this into consideration. Me, I am a Russian Jew, born and brought up in China. For which government do they imagine I spy?'

'Where do you get this very virile and deceptively mild-tasting vodka from, then, old beano?'

'Um, mmm, hmmm, from the Russian embassy – just a friend, you know, darling, actually the cultural attaché.'

'Ahhh, would you be kind enough to let Hussein and me have a little taste of it, then?'

'Darling, for you anything.' Shura moved away, iceward bound and casting anxious glances at Dom, Hussein and me, visibly invoking some Chinese god to preserve the peace and warmth of his house.

Dom uncurled from the comfortable bog of a large armchair. 'Hello,' he purred.

'Quite so. Hello.' Have you met Hussein Shariffe . . .? Dom Moraes.'

Hussein performed an elegant little dance and Dom refilled his glass and sank back into the armchair, where he almost succeeded in becoming invisible.

On a small table lay an old, probably defunct pistol or musket. It was an interesting-looking piece. I picked it up, flourished it about a little, it had a good solid, reliable feel to it. I struck a few poses – what I imagined to be the stance of a classical musketeer or cavalier in combat. Meanwhile some sort of polite conversation took place in the background. I suddenly noticed that Dom had turned a sickly green and Shura and Hussein had the giggles.

'It's not loaded, of course, is it, Shura, darling?' Raised eyebrows. 'Hussein, shall we leave, do you think?'

★

Hussein was a Sudanese, the great great grandson of the mystical and magical Mahdi who defeated and decapitated the British hero General Gordon. Hussein had just come down from Cambridge. He wanted to be a painter and was most influenced by Paul Klee. His use of colour was quite different to Klee's and always reminded me of 'the sand of the desert is sodden red', etc. His family did not fully approve his choice of career. Hussein told me that once at a Cambridge party his host blandly introduced him to a young man called David Gordon.

'David Gordon, meet Hussein el Shariffe el Mahdi el Mamoun el Shariffe.'

After a preliminary stare of shocked amazement and a bit of stuttering . . . 'I say, you're not the Gordon that my great grandpa . . .'

'Well, yes, actually . . .'

They toasted each other and pondered on the strange and mysterious ways of the Lord.

Hussein came and stayed for quite a long time at Apollo. Nana loved him. His presence provoked a series of psychic phenomena. I was already aware of some odd goings-on. I would be reading in bed alone and would often think that I heard the sound of footsteps in the studio next door to my bedroom. Maybe Dom coming home late after some toot or other. I'd get up to welcome him and find the studio completely empty.

I'd booted the tenant in the flat downstairs out. He was an old friend called Daniel Sykes. He was in a bad way and I liked him, but he couldn't pay the rent and I needed it to keep the household together. I put an advertisement in the same old paper shop round the corner in the King's Road and three pretty Canadian-Chinese girls arrived.

'Yes, you can have it. It's ten pounds a week. If that's OK by you, it is by me.'

'My God,' they said, 'you're the first person we've been to who has said yes to us. It's because we're Chinese.'

The morning after the first night they had moved in they said, 'That was a hell of a party you had last night. We wish you'd asked us. We couldn't sleep because of the racket going on, dancing about and singing and music and all.' I was stunned. I'd spent the evening alone, reading, and had gone to bed at about eleven.

I was puzzled but not frightened. I felt no sort of personally directed antagonism. I felt, in essence, that the house and I loved each other. Nana told me that she often saw a strange man wandering about in the hall downstairs, but she wasn't bothered about him, either. The psychic activity was at its height in the summer, especially in July and August. One evening I was going out. I was dressed in the height of fashion: late Fifties; a very full skirt, tightly belted and with layers and layers of different-coloured petticoats. As I stood at the top of the studio stairs waiting for the doorbell to ring, I heard the sound of heavy footsteps mounting the stairs, down which I was looking. I could see nothing and was rooted to the spot with fear. As the steps reached my level, the leaves of my skirt were pushed aside and the invisible energy passed by me.

Nana's only son, her beloved Georgie, was repainting the studio walls. He was alone one summer evening. Suddenly he threw down his paint brush and fled. 'Why did you do that, Georgie?' He explained that he had become aware of an unidentifiable but terrifying presence around him.

When Hussein arrived, things hotted up. He saw the sofa breathing as if it were an animate creature, he saw a man

68

sitting in an armchair, and he saw the classic African phenom-
enon of a bucket of blood containing a decapitated head. One
night Hussein and I were lying in bed just on the edge of
sleep. I opened my eyes and saw a dirty, sulphurous yellow
light hovering in the air on the other side of the room near the
bedroom door. I froze with terror. I knew that if the light
touched either of us, we would die. It was deadly evil, dancing
and hovering about but gradually drawing nearer. I thought,
Be careful, check it with Hussein, it could be a hallucination.

'Hussein, can you see anything odd in this room? Please
look around.'

He said, 'Yes. There's a dangerous-looking light in the
corner over there.'

I turned on the bedside lamp. There was nothing. I turned it
off and the danger returned, so I switched it on again.

Hussein said to me, 'Now, listen carefully to me. Have you
been doing anything, anything at all that you shouldn't have
been?'

I did a re-run, nothing came up. 'No, I haven't, I'm sure of
that. The thing is, Hussein, I believe that if that thing over
there touches us, we will die, sure as eggs is eggs. It's after us,
isn't it? What shall we do? It goes away when the light is on.
Let us pray to God to take it away from us.' So we prayed.
Hard.

'Do you think it's OK to turn the light off now?' I asked
him after a while.

'Yes.'

I did so. The room was calm and peaceful again and we fell
asleep.

I decided to do some research on the history of 9 Apollo
Place. I loved it and it loved me, I was sure of that. Johnny's

spirit, full of love and goodwill, was always present. I talked to Nana about it. She agreed that the manifestations were certainly genuine but that they had nothing to do with us. I found from one source or other that the first African slaves to come to England had been brought up the Thames as far as Turner's Reach and chained up in warehouses opposite and later sold. Many of them died. My house joined up with Turner's house, which fronted on to Cheyne Walk, number 118, and which at one point had belonged to Mrs Fleming who had made the beautiful garden that my studio windows looked out upon. This whole area had originally been the site on which the warehouses for the slave-trade traffic had stood. All became clear and I asked Peter Levi, who by then had become an ordained priest, if he could exorcize the house for me. Alas, he told me, 'Although we do believe and practise the rite of exorcism, we do not believe in the reality of ghosts.' My mind boggled wildly at this but after Hussein had gone away everything quietened down. After all, he was an African and a Sudanese, and they were great slave-traders.

Chapter Nine

One afternoon I was having a drink in the French Pub with Francis Bacon and Deakin and others. Francis said, 'I'm thinking of painting some of my friends and I'd like to do you but I can really only work from photographs, so, if it's OK, Deakin will come round to your house and take them. I'll tell him what I want. You are beautiful, darling, and you always will be, you mustn't worry about that.'

Deakin arrived at Apollo a few days later. We had some drinks and a little bit later retired to my bedroom.

Deakin said, 'He wants them naked and you lying on the bed and he's told me the exact positions you must get into.' Feeling a little shy of stripping in front of someone who definitely did not desire me and for all I knew might never have seen a female body in its entirety, might even be disgusted by it, I sat on the edge of the bed with my arms and legs crossed.

'For God's sake, sweetie, that's not exactly inspiring. I mean, he's not into the Pietà phase.'

'Well what shall I do, then?' I squeaked.

'Throw yourself back on to the bed and abandon yourself. Open up your arms and legs wide. Come on.' He started snapping wide-angle shots between my legs.

'Deakin, I know you've got it wrong. Francis can't possibly want hundreds of shots of these most private parts in close-up. I just don't believe that is what he is interested in painting. It can't be so.' In the end, he overrode me. After all Bacon had told *him*, not me, what he was after and so forth. I had a couple more drinks and gave in.

'Oh, all right, then, go ahead. It's only images, after all.' Snap, snap, snap, and on and on he went.

'That's it,' he said finally.

'Yeah, I should think that you'd have just about covered every angle,' and eventually, 'Shall we go and have a drink?'

I was having a drink with Francis Bacon and Deakin in the Colony Room. Francis said, 'Look here, Henrietta, this blithering nitwit has reversed every single shot of you that I wanted.'

'Ho,' I said. 'You amaze and astonish me.'

'Well, look here, Henrietta —' Francis shot his cuffs, displaying enormously strong-looking wrists — 'would you mind letting him do the whole thing all over again, but the other way up this time?'

I gazed at him. When I was eighteen, I had spent almost all my mornings, afternoons and evenings with him, dined alone with him at Wheeler's, oysters and Chablis, gone with him to the Gargoyle, listened to the wit and wisdom which flowed almost continuously from his lips. Sometimes I was aghast at the scathing sarcasm which bubbled out of him, but it had never been directed at me. At every meeting I had learned something new from him, been captivated, spellbound. Wherever he appeared, the air brightened, groups of people were animated, electricity hummed and buzzed and bottles of champagne appeared. I had learned so much of the ways of the world from him and, though at that time I had not properly understood half of his teaching, it had nevertheless, willy-nilly, been assimilated.

'No, of course I don't mind. Any time.'

So Deakin and I had a reverse performance and this time it came out right. 'One day I'll give you a picture,' Francis said.

'Goody.' I thanked him, not understanding just how much it meant.

One afternoon, about a week later, I wandered into a Soho drinking club, a bit off my beat, but in I went. The room was full of sailors, all of them crowding round a familiar figure – Deakin. His hands were full of the original photographs he'd taken of me and he was selling them off for ten bob a time.

'Deakin,' I yelled at him, 'I don't care, really, but don't you think you should buy me a large drink?'

John Deakin was never at a loss. His leathery face grinning, he bought me several.

Every summer Nana used to take Joshua and Caroline to Ireland, to Arklow, to stay with her daughter Anna and her eleven children. This particular year she didn't come back. The children came back to go to school, but she wrote saying she'd like to stay on a bit longer. I thought nothing of it. I knew she loved her home town of Arklow and often missed it. The weeks passed and I had no more news. As autumn passed into winter, I began to wonder. One afternoon my friend Merilyn came to see me.

'Don't you think we had better go to Ireland at once?' she asked.

Certainty flooded me. 'Yes, of course, now,' I said.

We got to London airport. The runways were blocked with freezing snow and we waited in misery. In the car from Dublin to Arklow my uneasiness grew unbearably. I filled a little silk purse with money and wrapped up a bottle of John Jameson in green paper. When we got to the house, I steadied myself and went in. Nan lay, so tiny, in bed, her grey eyes enormous in her head, watching the door. She gave a little crow of joy. She was bone-dry and burning hot and very frail. We talked about our life together and how good it had been and we smoothed out the tiniest wrinkles that had ever marred its surface. When I gave her the purse she smiled, but when I offered her some whisky she refused.

'Are you in pain, darling?' I asked her.

'No, no, but I feel very strange, Hennyietta, and I'm dying of thirst.'

When we left that evening, I went to see her doctor. 'Please tell me what is the matter with Mrs Grice, please, doctor.'

'Well now, Mrs Moraes, she has cancer.'

'And can nothing be done for it, anything, anything?'

'Well, you see now, my dear, she's riddled with the thing and there's nothing to be done.'

I went back to the hotel with Merilyn and wept. Great wracking sobs that went on for a long time, that hurt. The pain and regret that accompanies the loss of a loved person who loves without reserve. We spent the next day together and managed to achieve a sort of gaiety, then we left. The next morning Nana died. She was fifty-four years old.

★

My good star had departed . . . and, with it, my stability. That was the end of my youth – when Nana died and I later had to leave Apollo Place.

Chapter Ten

I dropped out. I started to retreat. One morning I woke up and, instead of leaping into the bath and off to work, I lay in bed and thought, To hell with it, I've had enough. I'm just not going to spend my life dreaming up ways to sell pens and cars and sausages and beans. I stayed in bed for six weeks, watching television and drinking Teacher's whisky – I believe I liked the name.

I picked up bad habits like a magnet does iron filings. I am erratic, neurotic, demanding, devious and fickle, subject to my emotions and moods. Sometimes I am wise after the event, seldom before it.

I had a boyfriend called Joe, who took drugs. I knew about taking purple hearts, from my doctor, and I'd smoked some grass. Joe was a registered drug addict and at that time could obtain his drugs from his doctor. He used about thirty grains of heroin a day and about fifty grains of cocaine. There wasn't too much pressure on a junkie in those days: he was just another patient in the doctor's surgery and just another customer collecting his National Health prescription in the chemist's shop. The eccentric behaviour of these individuals in these environments could be remarked upon, of course. A stocky but wiry lady vaulted over the dispensary counter of John Bell & Croyden one night and made off with two large bottles before the hard-working dispenser could turn round. Certain doctors' surgeries were crowded with scruffy men with running noses, shivering fits and a grand impatience to get in to the doctor. But there was no real stigma and only a very small black market in hard drugs.

Some of Joe's friends started coming round to Apollo. They intrigued me – that they could sit around all day long just shooting stuff into their veins, one fix after another. I couldn't imagine it. Tony, an orphan, who had been in and out of institutions all his life, Dirty Junkie Joyce, who lived in a dustbin halfway between her doctor's surgery and her chemist in Fulham Road. Once the visits started, a sort of intimacy was forged. The odd person stayed the night and then another, till suddenly it seemed like some ancient hospital.

I wrote an article for the *Sunday Times* about junkies. It was factual, fairly lightweight material, except for the obvious fact that most of these people had reached a sociological rock-bottom; it did not explore the more profound psychological factors for addiction. Keeping myself apart from the needle, I stepped up my pill-taking – no trouble from the doctor – and imagined that some sort of gulf divided me from them. The pills took the edge off life, as it were.

I was unable to keep up the mortgage repayments on Apollo and finally the inevitable foreclosure arrived. I sold the house to a young doctor and with great grief in my heart I departed to the other side of Battersea Park. I bought a

Victorian mansion flat in Prince of Wales Drive, which runs alongside Battersea Park, knocked down some walls to create more space, put in central heating and a telephone, sanded and polished the floors and attempted to reorientate. Joshua and Caroline went to the same school in Chelsea, crossing the park merrily each morning.

I continued to write articles, curiously drawn towards subjects of a morbid or pathological nature – women alcoholics, drugs and a quasi-religious therapeutic movement. It interested me because it had made so much money. I met some of its casualties – highly intelligent, rich parents, public school, who had put themselves unreservedly in the hands of this movement and were all suffering from some form of nervous breakdown or were incarcerated in mental hospitals. I wrote a rough draft for the *Sunday Times* which was approved, got my expenses and an advance and went ahead. I went to their headquarters every day for several months, resolutely refusing the offer of free processing (rather like cheese, I thought) and gradually a picture of some horror was revealed to me. The movement insisted on total obedience, secrecy and the shedding of all old ties including family ties. There was a form of crude treatment in which the subjects' reactions were read on a very simple galvanometer (lie detector). This was used to establish the veracity of the movement's dogma over the erring individual. What it all amounted to was an effective form of brain-washing, with the consent of the victim, who of course was unaware of the nature of the beast, and, to add insult to injury, was paying very stiff fees for it. It is a fact that a continued verbal assault on an individual will weaken the established brain patterns and new patterns can be imposed. With a considerable amount of guile and hard work, I finished the article and trotted off triumphantly to the *Sunday Times*. I considered this writing to be new and important, but it was rejected as being too 'cranky' – just another movement which wouldn't last and, anyway, the people in it were just freaks. Outraged, I did the rounds. Same thing everywhere, rejection. It has been said that any work of occult import will always be suppressed, for a time. Eventually I fell in with the lads from *Oz*, Richard Neville and Martin Sharp, and they gladly took it.

One afternoon I came home unexpectedly to find two tightly belted, mackintoshed figures bending over my typewriter and leafing through my manuscript. They were henchmen from the movement. They swung round as I entered the room. One of them pointed his finger at me. 'You will never write again,' he enunciated.

Though no one, especially myself, was aware of it, I entered a state of acute amphetamine psychosis, a condition of severe mental derangement caused by the habitual use of amphetamines. Burglary became my obsession, cat burglary. Not so much for the gain of possessions, for they were nothing more than the endless bric-à-brac collected by a human jackdaw, but for the breathless excitement to be had from breaking and entering another's stronghold – the exhilaration of shinning up a drainpipe, sliding through an open window, tip-toeing through an occupied bedroom and making off with a couple of bathroom towels and a brass ashtray. I adored the danger. I had a partner in crime, Stan, a friend of Joe's. He was more of a professional and knew all sorts of little tricks and dodges, but he had his weaknesses.

One night in late May Stan and I went to Hampstead to

have a drink with an acquaintance of mine. We drank a fair bit, smoked some hashish and took our regular dose of pills. We left at about half past three in the morning. It was a beautiful May night, warm and fragrant, and there was a full moon. As we walked through the Vale of Health, feeling on top of the world, Stan jumped in the air every so often, coming to earth with a portable radio in his hand, a bunch of flowers, a drink.

We came to the gateway of a large neo-Georgian mansion, which gave the impression of being lived in by some prosperous company accountant.

'In we go,' said Stan.

'Perfect,' I replied nonchalantly.

We entered the house noiselessly through the French windows. Stan had some trick using the abrasive side of a matchbox. There was a bar. We sat on the leather stools and had a few cocktails. I collected a few odds and ends and put them in one of my shopping baskets – my handbag, letters and diary were in the other – and we were away. Our haul included a couple of Meissen saucers, a child's Stradivarius and a bottle of whisky wrapped up in a table runner. The sun had risen, it was a perfect day.

As we walked up Church Row towards Hampstead Underground Station, home to safety and self-congratulation, Stan said, 'My God, I ain't 'alf 'ungry.' He pointed to a pork chop sitting behind bars in a ground-floor kitchen window. ''Ang on, girl, won't be long.'

'No, no, Stan,' I muttered too late. He'd vanished. I hung about, baskets in hands, shifting from one foot to the other nervously. I was just about to leave well alone when the front door was flung open to reveal Stan carrying a large ladies' handbag. Behind him loomed a florid figure wearing blue and white striped pyjamas. As he tore past me, Stan threw the bag at me and hissed, 'Run, and when I say run, I mean, RUN!'

So I did, but not very well, being hampered by my swag baskets, which I could not relinquish because of my personal effects therein. And so, the familiar old nightmare began. I was running clumsily up the hill, carrying two heavy baskets, pursued by a rather corpulent middle-aged man dressed in his pyjamas, shouting the words, 'Stop, thief!' My legs felt more and more leaden and I got a stitch in my side. I could hear him panting a few yards behind me. Stan had long since vanished in a puff of smoke. The milkman paused to take in this scene, put his bottles down on the pavement and joined in the chase. So did the newspaper delivery boy, who threw his bike into a hedge. Finally, the blow fell, a heavy hand slammed down on my shoulder, and a voice said, 'Got you.' I tried to talk him out of telephoning the police – after all I hadn't been in his flat – but when his wife saw her handbag in my basket that settled it. Two squad cars arrived and a long lanky policeman who looked a bit like George Formby said, 'You don't know what time of day it is, do you, darling?' It was ten past eight in the morning, for God's sake.

In the station I underwent some heavy grilling. My accomplice, who was he? I refused to answer. It didn't matter because Stan had just been caught trying to break and enter my flat. I made my one permitted telephone call to my doctor. By the time he arrived from Camberwell with some money it was too late to go to court and be granted bail and, short of approaching a judge in chambers, there was nothing to be done. I went off to Holloway in a Black Maria.

We were shown into Reception, stripped, examined medically, for crabs as far as I could make out, put into a bath, bundled into a threadbare prison dressing-gown and locked up in a sort of wooden hen coop for a couple of hours. Some poor souls had evidently thought that this was it, for there were various messages scrawled on the sides: 'Abandon hope' and 'Dear God, please help me now'. Unlocked and herded into a queue – I think I was probably mixed up with convicted prisoners – I was handed some ill-fitting clothes for the night: one pair of different-sized shoes, bra, stockings, a blue cotton overall and a shameful pair of knickers like corrugated iron. A wardress led me back through Reception, twirling a large bunch of keys. She stopped in front of a steel door and opened it. We stood at the end of one of the eight radials which form the spider's web pattern of Holloway gaol. The smell of fear and hysterical unhappiness hit me in the nostrils. There were sounds of shouting, crying, blaspheming and the racket of tin plates being hammered on the cell doors. I looked up politely. 'I can't possibly go in there,' I said. 'It's like feeding time at the zoo. Please take me somewhere else.' I was booted in and locked up in a matchbox with a tiny square window high up in the wall. I put the chair on the table and climbed on to it and looked out. The citizens of Pentonville Road, Holloway, outlined in black against their yellow window-panes, ate their fish and chips, drank their cups of tea, smoked their cigarettes. I resigned myself to the mounting and grotesque claustrophobia within and without – the matchbox was now the size of a sugar cube – climbed on to my bed and waited for the morning and release.

The magistrates' court referred our case to a higher court, the Inner London Sessions. Because we were in Hampstead, over six miles away from our place of residence, our crime was technically a much graver offence than if we'd been caught in someone else's house in Prince of Wales Drive. I had a solicitor and a lady barrister, whom unfortunately the judge did not seem to care for. Not for one minute did I take this case seriously, it never entered my head that I would be found guilty. Reality and I were poles apart. Stan had a solicitor and barrister too. Stan and I were at daggers drawn: I thought he'd let me down and vice versa. Somehow our counsels made this the main issue of their defence and each spent his time trying to disprove any statement made by the other's client and generally vilifying our characters to each other, the judge, the jury, the clerk of the court and the public gallery. I found this amusing and got into the swing of it, played my lines for laughs and got them from my friends in the gallery. Looking at the judge's empurpled face as he delivered his judgement I felt apprehensive. Stan got two years and I got a fortnight's remand in custody for a medical report and the rest was left as a question mark for the time being.

Back to Holloway, but this time I was only bored by the initial procedure and pleasantly surprised to find myself in a ward in the hospital wing with other prisoners, among them an acquaintance. Even so, I had no cigarettes and it took me three days to pluck up the nerve to demand one – you do not ask politely in prison, you demand. Never has time passed so slowly. With great control I refrained from looking at the clock for what I reckoned to be three quarters of an hour. Five and a half minutes had passed. The main problem was to keep out of trouble in order to get a good medical report. The place was rather like my first convent. Naturally the hospital was full of nutters, including three murderesses. One of these was only sixteen years old. She had strangled a boy of twelve on the Sussex Downs because she had felt like it, she told me. She prowled around like a tiger, on the balls of her feet, sometimes attacking those around her for no apparent reason.

We worked hard, packing plastic spoons for cinema ice-creams. The Borstal girls at the back used to pack theirs up their knickers first, so I have never eaten an ice-cream since then – that is, not in my local cinema. The Borstal girls were a fiery, independent, non-institutionalized group, so they were often in trouble with the screws. The hospital wing was rightly considered dangerous work. Two male warders from Pentonville were always on duty. One was small, pale-faced, and could have been a poet; the other was short, squat, red-faced with a military moustache. The poet-face was always beating up young girls for being cheeky; the sergeant-major would slip you a rolled-up fag if you looked desperate. Quite a high proportion of the Borstal girls suffered from epileptic fits. All would be quiet in the workroom, when suddenly a scuffle would start in the back rows, a few thuds and grunts and then the sight of a teenage girl from Brixton lying on her back, eyes rolling, straddled by a screw, with a baton clenched between her teeth to stop her from swallowing her tongue.

I had been in prison for a few days when I was summoned to see my probation officer. I went with some trepidation to meet my possible nemesis. A female intellectual version of Dougal, of the *Magic Roundabout*, greeted me. 'Henrrrrrrietta, I only want to put your mind at rest. I know how you must be feeling. Is it the sword of Damocles?' I nodded mutely. 'Well now, since you seem such a sensible sort of person, I shall recommend probation to the judge. I don't think prison's the right place for such as you.' I was fairly astonished by this bland assumption of power over the normal legal processes; I suppose I goggled. 'Oh, don't you worry, Henrrrrrrietta, I'm telling you the truuuuth.' Very much reassured, I thanked Miss Patterson from the bottom of my heart and, sure enough, at the end of the fortnight I was given two years' probation and put in the care of this extraordinary Scottish humanist.

I don't know about the others, but I do know about Miss Patterson, who displayed the utmost kindness and depth of perceptive understanding towards me in the next two years. She chided me, protected me, asked me to lunch, cared for my children and was always ready for a good laugh: a lovely woman.

One afternoon in early summer, my children and I were wandering through Battersea funfair. Joshua adored the rifle ranges and bingo; Caroline and I, the paratrooper and the dodgems. We were watching the progress of the Big Dipper, which was manned by an extraordinary figure riding the brakes on the outside of the car and whooping, hallooing and shouting strange calls. We were interested.

Not long after I came home from Holloway I was offered an ampoule of methedrine, which I eagerly accepted. Methedrine is a form of liquid amphetamine, for injection, and it is very, very strong. It was once used to resuscitate the dead by injection straight into the heart. I am told that Hitler was fond of it and it was used by military personnel who needed to perform irksome tasks tirelessly and without fear. The Japanese post-war industrial boom was said to have been the result of factory workers' wages paid in the minimum yen and the maximum methedrine. Be all that as it may, I know only that the first injection of methedrine that I ever had – a combination of the time and the circumstances, of course – lifted me up on

to a wave and I coasted home at the speed of light on its crest:
the duck to water.

One afternoon I went to Oakley Street to score – I hadn't
got round to admitting I needed a doctor yet. I went up into
this girl called Eleanor's room. It was about twelve feet by
nine and it held twenty or so people, all trying to score or,
having scored, trying to have a fix. I made a successful bid
and, having concluded my business, loosened the tie on my
arm and looked up, straight into the eyes of the boy who'd
been driving the Big Dipper. He was looking at me with such
fervent longing that I got up and crossed the few feet to where
he was leaning up against the wall. He was massively built,
like a black bull, with dark clusters of curls hanging over his
forehead, black silver-studded leather clothes, winkle-pickers,
hands in pockets. He leaned desperately against the wall.

'Do you want some of this stuff?' I asked him and he
nodded. 'Do you want me to do it for you?' Again he nodded.

Afterwards he sighed and said, 'That's the first time.'

Horrified, I said, 'Well, in that case you are to come home
with me and I'll look after you.' Since he was living in a
number 19 bus in the Battersea depot he agreed. His name was
Rebel and he came from South Africa, Section Six in Cape
Town, a particularly notorious district where the 'Cape col-
oureds' were herded together. Rebel's first memory was of
having his head kicked in by a policeman when he was about
four years old. He had this job in Battersea funfair and a friend
called Angelo, a gypsy from Warwickshire.

Of course, the opposite thing happened to what I intended.
Rebel looked after me. He moved into a little room at the end
of the flat and swept and polished and washed and disciplined
the dog, Chloe, and played with the children. 'Rebel, yippee,

teach us how to fight with a knife.' The soul of gentle willingness in the home and with an extraordinary insight into the human character, he was a tiger with the rest of the world. The boys in the funfair used to work one or more quarrels between themselves every week, and each Saturday night they would fight it out with knives on a little patch of ground in the park just below Chelsea Bridge. Rebel had been a figure in these fights – in fact he told me that he had killed two boys. I made him promise never to do this again. I also made him give me his solemn word not to take more than two methedrine a day. He could easily have done so – there were enough doctors in London who would issue practically unlimited prescriptions for methedrine; some thought it preferable to cocaine. I felt that Rebel's mentality was too simple to deal with the complexity of the methedrine reaction and the megalomania that often resulted.

I was aware of the danger of this stuff – not that it put me off, but I took certain precautions. Every ten days I would give it up entirely just to see if I could and what it felt like. Well, I could and it didn't feel too bad, if I could stay in bed all day long. But as time went by, of course, it took me over. I didn't sleep for ten days once. I kept going until I keeled over into blackness, luckily in my bedroom. Life assumed a dream quality, a mixture of *Marvel* comics and the occult. For three months the pleasure of this speeded-up existence was undiminished. No self-consciousness, no normal moral or ethical questions to consider and, above all, no self-examination and reproof. When Rebel, Angelo and I walked down the street, people would scatter and pavements clear before us. Rebel used to make some of my clothes, sort of soft black leather, very short skirts trimmed with white fur and silver, green and purple glitter. I accepted it all as a normal expression of an inward state of being.

One afternoon I was looking out of the drawing-room window at the boating lake in the park. It was twilight and the water was full of gleaming reflections of the trees and flowering bushes. Chinese ducks and swans paddled across the mirror surface and above them the rooks and the starlings were engaged in their nightly territorial arbitration. A knock at the door. I opened up and there stood a boy called Ivan the Fox and a friend. 'We're hungry,' he announced. 'Have you got any food?' I did have quite a lot of food, my aunt Jo had sent us a garrison-size food parcel that Christmas, so I loaded up two carrier bags of it for them. At the door, on his way out, the Fox looked at me obliquely. 'I'll be back later on.'

When he came back I was alone. The children were in bed, Rebel was in his room. Ivan put his hand in mine and slipped me an inch-square block of very black hashish. I put on a record, Brother Jack McDuff playing 'Silk and Soul', we each rolled a joint and lit up. He started tapping out a counter rhythm, something odd like 13/8 on a 6/4 tempo. He rose and circled round the room gracefully, a sort of hedge-hopping flight. I joined him and we soared up high above Trafalgar Square. I lay down on the blue-brocaded sofa and, suspended from an arch, I watched a red cube slowly revolve, it had the number 15 inscribed on it in glowing crimson figures. I got a jolt and sat up.

'You've come to tell me that Rebel is going away, haven't you?'

Ivan looked at me sorrowfully. 'Poor Rebel,' he said, 'he's not very well.'

At this moment I saw Rebel at the end of the passage. He

was silhouetted in the doorway of his room, his arms looked abnormally long and he was crouching on his knees.

I was studying tarot cards and when I did a reading, I often worked with Rebel – I found his presence gave me extra intuitive power.

He said, 'Will you do my tarot?'

I felt a great reluctance. 'No, I don't want to, Reb.'

'Let's do a tarot on Roderick.'

'Do you think?' I said. 'He's not here.'

'Well, we'll tell him,' said Rebel.

'OK.' I laid out the cards, paused . . . aghast. 'He's going to die, he's surrounded by death, it's ridiculous, I don't believe it and yet . . .'

Rebel pored over the cards but said nothing. It was only much later that I realized that I had used the same card to represent Roderick that I would have used for Rebel, their birthdays being close to one another.

I never left the flat for any length of time without Rebel, except once. I went out to dinner with a friend of mine. Rebel seemed a little distressed.

'You're not going out tonight, are you?'

'Yes, Reb. I haven't been out to dinner for ages. I won't be long.' In the event I was far too long because when I came back Rebel was dead. He died of heart failure.

People were dying off like flies round me. The strain on the heart was too great and it failed.

My children went to stay in the house of Doctor Geoffrey Gray in Beaufort Street. They were looked after by a friend of mine, an opera singer called Bickerstaff. Miss Patterson arranged their entrance into a school called Frensham Heights.

Because my life had become unmanageable, I accepted these arrangements, but I know now that my children suffered a lot and if I could change anything in my life it would be this.

I started to go to a clinic in Chelsea run especially for methedrine users. The cliquishness and snobbery among drug users are as great as in any other social stratum and there was little mixing between the clans. This clinic was run by the Salvation Army and it was in the World's End. We were given two ampoules of methedrine a day by the doctor: one to get us there in the morning and one to keep us out of trouble in the evening. We were also given lunch, a very good idea because that was all most of us ever had to eat. The honeymoon period had been over for some time for me. I couldn't take off any more – in fact, more often than not I couldn't even find a vein in my arms willing to bear an injection. Veins retreat from the surface if they are abused. Then my blood started clotting in the syringe and I was unable to inject on this account. All in all, things were at a very low ebb, and yet it still didn't occur to me to try and stop. Nobody ever suggested it.

One day, I was on my way from World's End to Park Walk to see a friend of mine when I lost consciousness three times in three hundred yards. I suddenly made up my mind. 'If I can get where I'm going, I'm going to give up methedrine.'

The door opened. 'Oh, Philboy, could I please stay here a few days and just go to bed? I'm afraid I'm rather ill but I'll be all right.'

'Yes, yes,' said Philboy kindly and showed me upstairs to a bedroom. I got into bed and went to sleep.

I woke up. It was dark and I was deathly cold. A black wind was blowing through the marrow of my bones. I hadn't the energy, strength or willpower to raise a finger on my hands. So I just lay there in convulsions of cold. 'I'll do it for Rebel,' I thought viciously. Three days later I got up and had a bath. All my skin peeled off like a snake in springtime. On the fourth day I felt as if a strong, stiff, dusty, grey cobweb was slowly unfolding from my brain. It seemed to creak as layer after layer was separated, dead, dried flies and dust falling away; the pink, exposed brain cells, pulsating underneath, seemed very vulnerable. On the tenth day I was feeling more myself. I put on a moss-green velvet suit bought in Granny Takes a Trip – it had a Royalist lace collar – and went for a walk down the King's Road. Three wolf whistles from three lorry drivers restored me to the human race.

Chapter Eleven

The weakest point in the spiritual armour of anyone who has begun to reform or to change the pattern of their life is the sudden awareness of time, a lot of time on one's hands. This is where confusion, indecision and temptation lie.

It was 1966 and there were the strains of a prolonged party in the air. I heard them faintly at first. 'I say, there's an extraordinary new thing about, it's called acid. It's not exactly a drug. Anyway, you take it on a sugar cube and go to heaven or something.' Or, 'Michael took a trip and met Sir Lancelot at the foot of Glastonbury Tor.' There was a new look on the streets. Long-silky-haired youths and girls dressed in silks, satins, ribbons and laces, gentle smiles on radiant faces, festoons of flowers. One saw a sort of esoteric kind of camaraderie. Verbal exchanges were soft, slow and in a new form of language. 'Hallo, man, meet my chick. You know this is where it's all at.'

It was a fine, hot summer and the parks and squares of London were filled with groups of young people sitting on the grass, sometimes playing musical instruments, smoking joints, eating health food picnics – as pretty a pageant as any medieval saint's day. The American 'hipster' had been translated into the more innocent English 'hippie'. Yipeeeeee ... it really was playtime. Almost everyone of my circle downed tools, if ever they'd taken them up, and abandoned work. Luckily, the hippie code that evolved stressed that money was the root of all evil, all men were brothers and that man was made in the image of God. This code embraced all religions.

I went to see my dear friend Bill one evening. An American beauty of Irish descent, he was the possessor of the legendary emerald-green eyes, the narrow, slanting cheekbones and the glossy black hair of Erin's fair isle. He asked me if I would like to accompany him to his bathroom. Sure, I would. I sat down with some formality on a white chair. He explained the origins of a beautiful white silk shawl lying on a little sofa, picked up a four-litre bottle of colourless liquid and said, 'Would you like to try this? It's called lysergic acid, LSD 25. I've just flown in from Switzerland with it. I went to a laboratory called Sandoz, who sold it to me. It's been synthesized by a doctor called Hoffmann who's been working on it for years. It's a hallucinogen and it's being used by doctors to work on the psyche of some of their patients. It's pure acid, baby.'

He half filled a medicine dropper with the colourless liquid and approached, holding it high in the air. I opened my mouth, received the drops on my tongue and to my astonishment said, 'Hit me again, father, I haven't done this for a very long time.'

Obediently, Bill half filled the dropper again, administered and screamed, 'Oh my Gahhhhhhhhhhhhhhhhhhd! . . . What have I done? That's about 6,000 micrograms.'

I didn't care what he'd done. The scales were falling off my eyes and they were opening on to a new world. I'd no idea that the world was so beautiful. Like Aldous Huxley, I'm a literary person rather than a visual one, I even dream in manuscript form, pages and pages of sepia manuscript, flowing quill-penned lines in Aramaic, and in my dreams all written by me. Now, all around me was shimmering and sparkling, the colours of objects became alive like flower petals, the flowers in the vases breathed gently. Candles in their engraved-glass reflections glowed warmly and their haloes were like rainbows. On a large, bare, white wall opposite an exquisite show of oriental carpets, the patterns, colours and textures reforming into new displays constantly. Outside the windows, Cheyne Walk lay dark and mysterious and the river shone with all the lights from Battersea funfair reflected like fireworks in its depths.

I looked at Bill, he had turned into Katharine Hepburn. I stared.

'Why are you looking at me like that? All my friends look at me like that when they are tripping.'

'Well, you've turned into Katharine Hepburn.'

A tall, pale young hero entered the room. He was dressed in a ruffled shirt, black knee breeches, white silk stockings and pumps. Curiously, he was lame in both legs. I went up to him and took a good look. 'You are far too heroic for me,' I remarked pleasantly. He was followed by Robert Fraser, who was dressed normally enough but sported a pair of horns, a dull orange halo which spat yellow sparks, a tail which lashed tightly to and fro, and a pair of cloven feet. Bill fed me with glasses of apple juice and saucers of raisins, the perfect food. The room was strewn with silken, silvery cobwebs, glittering with diamond drops. 'Watch out,' I thought to myself. 'Good evening, Robert.'

There was a move to go out, to go to a discotheque, to go to Blaises. When we got there, I was disturbed by the topographical confusion that I encountered at every turn. Alicelike, I paused in front of a door that was only two and a half feet tall, everything was made of looking-glass, we kept on falling through the floor on to a different movie set, once pursued by cowboys, once by pirates and once by desert raiders on camels. Eventually we sat down at a table and Robert ordered wine. The heat was equatorial, I was pouring with sweat, the wine arrived, it was brought by an Arab. I drank some. 'Robert, the Beaujolais is boiling hot.'

I walked home through Battersea Park, hup over the railings, over the grass and into the secret little rose garden tended by fierce lesbians. The trees were wreathed in trailing garlands of dripping purple flowers, it looked like Tahiti to me. I watched entranced as it grew lighter. The birds started to sing and, sitting on a little wooden bench in the south-east corner, overhung with the June roses, I watched the sun rise up to a perfect summer morning.

Lysergic acid is mainly non-toxic and leaves the blood stream clean in a few hours. It is believed to bridge the synapses, or the gaps in the non-connected areas of the brain and therefore of the consciousness. One becomes aware of different dimensions of reality, things hitherto hidden. Temporarily, new circuits can function and awareness is increased, sometimes to a great degree. The effect can be extremely confusing or frightening. For the majority, it can be an overwhelming experience – too much too quickly, as it were – and it should be used only the presence of an intelligent person who has considerable experience in both taking it and watching its effect on others. We, needless to say, observed none of these elementary precautions. We knew no better and I think we made the mistake of assuming that, because some profound change had occurred within ourselves, it was a permanent change and that the rest of the world had, or would, change with us. Fantasy ran riot.

I re-met the tall, pale young hero. His name was Stas de Rola. 'Please take off your shoes,' I begged him.

'But why?' He stopped to take off his shoes, two perfectly formed, rather noble-looking feet.

'I'll tell you . . .'

'Ah well, you see, I do think about Lord Byron quite a lot. I am descended from him.'

So acid lets you see what people are thinking about, does it?

Chapter Twelve

My life had changed enormously since I had given up methedrine. I certainly spent less and less time in my flat in Battersea. I couldn't quite bear the junkies that I'd harboured for so long, disliked the flat which had unhappy memories and no children in it. I was afraid of the place really.

I made an almost entirely new circle of friends, young and beautiful, worldly but innocent. They were the children of a privileged world and they were refreshing. I threw myself into their life and they seemed to quite like me, at any rate I became a fixture. The people I saw most of were Christopher Gibbs, the antique dealer, and David Mlinaric, called 'Monster', the interior designer; I mention these two first because they were the only two who seemed to work consistently and every day. I made friends with Michael and Jane Rainey and her sister Victoria and brother Julian; Christopher Sykes; Beatrix, Rose and Anne Lambton; Deborah and Angus Wood; Penny Cuthbertson, Mark Palmer and Catherine Tennant, who later married Mark; and many, many others.

★

The first two weeks of June are traditionally the most beautiful of the year and it was at this time that someone would hire a barge and about ten of us would embark on a canal holiday. The sun would shine, the water would glisten, the swans would glide, the rushes would sway, the dogs would bark, I'd light up a joint and we'd be off. One year, when we'd only been afloat for some two minutes, Jane and Victoria's father, who had masterfully taken the tiller, steered straight into another boat and we'd done a thousand pounds' worth of damage in a trice.

We always had a lot of dogs. I had a lurcher who was like a black greyhound: he was idle, beautiful and wicked and a tremendous sheep killer, I'm afraid, and came to a bad end. I also had a dear little yellow World's End mongrel bitch called Chloe. We made a tremendous racket as we progressed; Boots Bantock's sheepdog Bronwen could never stop barking, which set off the others, and they would all race up and down along the canal path accompanied by imperious cries of command from their owners.

One year I had been dropped off at a certain canal bridge by Michael Rainey and, as instructed, had descended to the path and turned right and started a ten-minute walk with my luggage and my dogs to where I would find the barge tied up for the night. I walked and I walked and I walked. I didn't wear a watch in those days. I went on and on until I saw the lights of a town some way ahead. It turned out to be Stratford. I was exhausted and the dogs and I went to sleep in a ladies' lavatory for a bit. Then I got up and retraced my steps back to the hump-backed bridge from where I had started and contin-ued in the opposite direction. I walked all night. The day dawned, the sun came up and still no barge. I was in despair and then I saw it, tied up on the other side of the canal! I was forced to cross by way of a railway bridge, very dangerous with the dogs who had no leads. A train came by just as I was starting, but eventually I arrived at the barge. I stumbled aboard, awaking the peaceful sleepers, seized a bottle of brandy provided by Tom Benson, the owner of Parkes restaurant, and told my tale to a gleeful audience.

One afternoon I was standing in the bows of the barge, smoking a joint and reading a book. I was comfortable and relaxed and, of course, not looking out. There was a tremendous bang. We had hit the side of the canal bank and I shot up in the air and over the side into the weedy water and underneath the barge. I thought my last moment had come and that I was about to be decapitated by the barge propeller which was more or less overhead, so I swam downwards vigorously like a frog till my lungs were bursting and eventually emerged still holding the book and smoking the joint.

In the evenings we would tie up in some luscious place, some luxuriant water meadow garlanded by willow trees, collect lots of wood and light an enormous fire. Some people, especially Monster, were very good at this and would build a huge cathedral-like structure.

Sometimes a very urban, uncertain-looking individual would arrive with a suitcase and sleeping bag. Peter Eyre was one such. I watched him shaking out his sleeping bag on the bank and solemnly winding up a large, rotund alarm clock and setting it by the pillow. He caught my eye and we had a fit of giggles.

One summer we went through Blisworth tunnel, which is over two miles long. Deborah and I sat on the roof; it was dank and dripped dismally on to us. It seemed an endless journey. The tunnel was very sad and haunted, and we thought of the Irish navvies who had built it. When at last we saw the bright light at the end, a tiny speck of sunlight, we were very happy. In the old days bargees would have to lie on their backs and paddle through with their feet. We travelled up the longest flight of locks, which took several hours of winding up and unwinding locks, opening and closing gates and waiting for the water to come in and go out. Happily most of this hard work was done by Alexi and Louisa, who had just started courting and were anxious to see the best of each other. We went over an immensely long and narrow viaduct which, to me, was terrifying. There seemed to be but a few inches of water and a very low wall separating us from the far distant land below.

Time on the canal seems immeasurable. Moving slowly along on a stretch of water through the imperceptibly changing countryside, having a completely new view of it all, transports you into a new dimension.

The last year was sad, though. It rained a lot and we had a series of minor accidents which culminated with an engine breakdown, alas.

Chapter Thirteen

By this time I had become a complete hippy. I dressed in Afghan robes and clothes from Hung on You, or crushed-velvet trousers and shirts with stars on them from Granny Takes a Trip. I got boots from Granny made in most fetching William Morris prints, chrysanthemum and honeysuckle. They laced up to the knee and, depending on how stoned I was, took at least ten minutes to put on. The Chelsea Cobbler sold a more elegant zip-up suede boot and I acquired a true Marvel comic pair in bright red and green, covered in gold stars, from Mr Freedom. I spent quite a lot of time shopping, going into the Antique Market to buy old Forties summer dresses, lace petticoats and embroidered shawls. The weather seemed to be summer always and there were varieties of acid about called Purple and Sunshine Yellow.

A girl called Sue started a café called the Flying Dragon in the World's End. It was dark inside, lit only by candles. There were small, round tables and lots of silk-embroidered cushions on the floor; chairs were OUT. It smelled of sandalwood, flowers and hashish. You could drink seven different kinds of tea, eat yoghurt and honey and talk to your friends all day long if you wanted to. There was a manager called Ed and a very handsome waiter called Guy. I had taken to 'crashing' in other people's 'pads'. This meant waiting till you were more or less the last person and saying, 'Can I crash in your pad, man?' This meant to spend the night.

Ed and Guy and I used to drop some acid late at night and go out for long walks around Chelsea. Dropping acid and smoking joints was to me, at that time, the equivalent of going to church. Taking these drugs was a spiritual exercise and I thought brought me nearer to the godhead. I certainly wasn't mad in the way that I had been before and I noticed that I was hardly drinking at all.

There were a lot of parties and Lara, a friend, held quite a few of them in her house in Cheyne Row. Victoria and I made such a strong chocolate hashish cake for Nicholas Gormanston's birthday that most of the guests became immobilized for twenty minutes or so. We would wander from house to house, from Christopher's flat in Cheyne Walk to Monster's studio in Tite Street to Bill's flat at the other end of Cheyne Walk and so on. We would drink apple juice, Schloer, smoke joints and talk, play Bob Dylan and the Rolling Stones and then go out to dinner at the Baghdad House and eat dates and hummus. It was in Monster's studio that I first noticed a very young and beautiful girl sitting on top of a high radiator, her legs dangling. She was evidently too shy to speak. I learned her name was Martha and after a bit she and Monster got married.

We danced a lot, facing not touching, and gyrating wildly as the mood and music took us. Deborah produced a lot of wonderful shirts in her shop in Beauchamp Place. They were mostly flower prints and everybody had some. Michael Rainey had some edible-looking, ice-cream-coloured suits in Hung on You – white, pink, pistachio-green and cream. These too were very popular. Moroccan burnouses and yellow babouches, shirts with lace ruffles at neck and cuffs, silks, satins, velvets, gypsy ear-rings, Indian rings and bracelets and, yes, even bells abounded.

One summer evening Brian Jones was drowned in his swimming pool and some little time afterwards the rest of the Stones gave a memorial concert at the Cockpit in Hyde Park. One of our friends, Suki, had lived with Brian and of course we decided to go to the park, along with twenty thousand other people.

I spent all the night and day before the concert with some acid-dealer friends wrapping up single trips in silver paper to distribute free to the crowds. We stuffed hundreds of them into the tops of our long boots and set out for the park. It was a most beautiful, late summer evening. Vast crowds were just beginning to collect when we arrived and we slipped through them to the front and staked our claim. Then we reached down into our boots, pulled out the little silver packets and threw them up into the sky, so that they glittered in the sunlight and caught the eye. 'Acid, acid, acid,' we called, like Christina Rossetti's goblins.

Eventually, Mick walked on to the stand and came up to the front. He was wearing white, a colour of mourning. It was a Michael Fish short white tunic dress with a very full skirt. He looked sad and he had an open book in his hand, out of which he read a short Shelley poem in honour of Brian. Then the music started, and for two and a half hours twenty thousand people sat and listened. They were as well behaved as any party from the Mothers' Union.

The only thing that really went wrong was that I lost my bitch, Chloe, and had to catch a train immediately after the concert. Tearfully, I told Martha and Monster who promised to try and find her. I departed, and Chloe turned up the next day in the care of the park police.

Chapter Fourteen

Mark Palmer sat in Hyde Park with Martin Wilkinson and Maldwyn Thomas. It was hot, it was crowded, it was full of people, it was London. An idea came. Why don't we drop out? Why don't we leave London and go to the country? Why don't we buy a horse and cart and travel all over the place, all over England in fact, like gypsies and be free? So that is what they did, and they travelled down to Port Eliot in Cornwall. They bought a gypsy barrel-top wagon and a brown and white coloured horse which they called Rizla, after the cigarette papers, and a brindled lurcher called Fly and off they went.

Several months later I was walking down the King's Road when I saw a tanned and exotic-looking Mark. 'Hello, hello.'

'Gosh, how lovely to see you.' I was never very cool.

'Are you coming to the country with us?'

'Who's "us"? Yes, of course I am. When are you going?'

Mark said, ' "Us" is Nigel Waymouth and Hapsash and the Coloured Coat, who have to get themselves together and get some new ideas. We've got to score something to smoke and some acid from Gerry, so we'll go tomorrow.'

Eight of us climbed into somebody's white car – Nigel, Terry, Greg, Nicky Kramer, John Pearse, Mark, Chloe and me. We started off for Trecarroll, near Launceston, sounds blaring, long hair blowing, feathers and silks furling in the wind.

'I don't think I'll take any acid till we get there,' I said modestly.

Everyone looked amazed. 'I should think not,' Mark said wryly.

Around midnight we had got as far as Devon. Further travel seemed unwise, so we stopped at a motel, progressed unnoticed to cabin 20, which was empty, and settled down for the night. Next morning an enraged 'mine host', drawn by the noise and laughter, erupted into the room and we left in rather a hurry, with promises to send the money on.

We arrived at Trecarroll Mill after midnight and dis-embarked. It was early in the year, Eastertime, and quite cold and wet. It was pitch-dark and the sky was without moon or stars. We started walking down a very muddy little path and into the woods. It was quite strange and I wondered where on earth Mark was taking us. I did not quite have the faith in him that I learned later. We walked for quite some time, the tree branches whipped back into my face. The little path curved and twisted and I fell over quite often and muddied my robe. At last, in a clearing and near the sound of a fast-running little river, I saw the shape of a gypsy wagon with glowing, lamplit windows illuminating a tethered brown-and-white horse and some lurchers who came out from underneath the wagon. Near by stood a tripod with a large cooking-pot hanging from it, the remains of a fire, a teapot, some mugs and a jar of honey. My heart swelled with pleasure and I thought, This is the life for me. Maldwyn shouted cosily from within and Mark climbed up the steps, paused at the door, turned round and said, 'There's an old shed over there you can all sleep in. I hope you've remembered your Kipwells. Goodnight.'

I was the first to wake up the next morning, a pattern which was to endure. I found myself lying damply in my sleeping bag on the ground. I was in a sort of dilapidated structure of gaping planks and corrugated iron which leaned sideways and looked unsafe. I groped about in my fringed and beaded Moroccan shoulder bag and rolled up a rather wet joint. As I smoked it, Nicky Kramer opened his eyes. 'Pass the joint,' he said.

I gathered up my clothes and emerged from the shack. It was paradise. We were camped in a sylvan glade, on a green velvet sward by the side of a bright and chuckling little stream which was full of smooth, rounded boulders and stones. The wagon was painted in the traditional fashion, maroon and gold. Rizla grazed peacefully on his tethering chain. I could see the gleaming grey coat of Sagittarius, Mark's Arab stallion, and some other horses through the trees. The dogs came out from under the wagon, stretching and yawning, their eyes alight with pleasure and welcome. Chloe looked at them with guarded interest. Fly was in pup, the latter stages.

I went downstream a bit, threw off my robe and stepped into the stream. I washed and cleaned my teeth, Sarakan toothpaste. I shook the mud off everything and got dressed, feeling like a new person. The newly opened, tender green leaves were as soft as cotton wool, the cushions of emerald-green moss sparkled in the sunlight. Tufts of primroses lined the riverbanks, fronds of bracken and bluebells poked through the ground, daffodils and aconites showed their shiny yellow heads and birds sang cheerfully everywhere. It was my first experience of a Cornish spring and I was enraptured.

I went for a walk and saw a vixen playing with her cubs on the other side of the river, small balls of red-gold rolling about. About a mile further up the valley I came to the house of Rob and Hope Stuart. They had Nicholas Gormanston staying with them and asked me to breakfast, which was civilized and pleasant.

'I hope you like it here, Henrietta,' Rob said proprietorially.

'I think it's the most beautiful valley in the world,' I said. 'I tell you what, though, Rob, do you think I could come and have a bath here every day, please?' He laughed and said of course I could.

Mark was very scornful when I told him this. 'Real travellers and people on the road don't have baths, Henrietta,' he said. 'What will you do when you really get going?' I thought I'd find a way and didn't reply.

On this visit we didn't move camp, so we didn't actually travel, but we did make an expedition to Launceston, a market town four miles away. We worked out that according to the legend this would be Lancelot's town and therefore of great interest. This expedition like all others, I realized gradually, entailed an enormous amount of preparation and time. First of all the horses had to be caught, groomed and harnessed up. Their shoes and feet had to be looked at. Rizla's tack had to be sorted out from the other harness, checked, polished a bit, and put on. To begin with only Mark and Maldwyn could do this, but eventually I learned too. It's quite a difficult job: the collar has to go over the horse's head, which is much taller than you are. It has to go on upside down or its head will not fit over the narrow part, and you have to reverse the collar once it's round the horse's neck. Then comes a really tricky manoeuvre: backing the horse between the shafts attached to the wagon so that it doesn't step on them and break them; lifting the shafts up and fitting them through the loops attached to the harness to connect the whole equipage. Most horses don't really like being backed up and make a bit of a fuss. Then various straps and buckles have to be adjusted and done up, pulled through and balanced, and at last you are ready.

On this occasion when Mark picked up the long reins and called out, 'Rizla!', obediently Rizla pulled forward, and a strap broke. Oh God. Start again.

I had been allowed to ride Sagittarius, bareback as Mark didn't believe in saddles or brakes. I got a leg up as nonchalantly as possible and we set off, as colourful a band of travelling gypsy musicians and squires as could be wished for. We caused a huge stir in Launceston. A lot of people thought we were the circus and tried to buy tickets from us. We bought some muesli and some lentils, some cigarette papers and some yoghurt. Mark bought some Mars Bars and I a *Daily Mail*.

We made various visits in the white car to local places connected with Arthurian legend: Camelot and Tintagel, where Arthur was said to be conceived, and Boscastle, where Merlin lived and where we saw a flying saucer quite close up.

I think Hapsash and the Coloured Coat must have got some inspiration. I know I did. I thought that my children would love the travelling life more than anything and I determined to introduce them to it as soon as possible. I too felt stifled in

London and resolved like Toad to take to the open road. With this in mind I climbed into the white car for the last time and set off for London and new plans.

Chapter Fifteen

All in all, the journey to Wales took four years, at an average speed of four miles a day. It wasn't supposed to be a practical journey, however, more in the nature of a quest.

Mark conceived it and led it and was there all the time, and so was Penny Cuthbertson with her wagon and her adorable coloured mare, Lily. Lily of the stout, hairy legs, cuddly body and indomitable spirit. Lily who loved a sugar cube.

Other people joined for a bit, came from London for the weekend. I was one who came and went, sometimes staying for quite long periods. In the school holidays I brought my children, Joshua and Caroline. They loved it, travelling the little roads with dogs and horses and gypsy wagons. What children would not?

The travellers spent their first winter in the stableyard of a house in Berkshire called Stargrove, then belonging to the great and indulgent Mick Jagger. Mick didn't live at Stargrove and the house was in the process of being refurbished and generally brought up to scratch by Christopher Gibbs. A lake and a cricket ground were wanted and the lake presented endless problems. Our great friend John Michell had often stayed in this house when a child and it was his opinion that if you played enough cricket on the ground to harden it and then flooded it, the lake would not drain away.

One day in early spring Catherine Tennant and I decided to pay a visit to Stargrove. When we arrived, it was bitterly cold with a hard frost on the ground. Dusk was falling and all was grey and eerie. The yard was deserted, so we went to the village and bought some cigarettes and Mars Bars. When we got back, Mark and Maldwyn and a boy called Mick had returned with some firewood and we greeted them and had a pipe of hash. Mark was very thin and pale and rather reserved. We spoke of the horses and Mark said that he wasn't riding just at the moment.

I felt uneasy. 'Why ever not?'

'Oh, um, boils . . .'

Boils! Why? What was going on? They must be very bad for Mark not to ride. We were worried and later on found we had reason to be. We had at the time a little-understood penchant for vegetarian and macrobiotic food, so we ate no meat and nothing white – bread, sugar, et cetera. We knew about green vegetables and their virtues but these were hard to get in a small village in the middle of March, so we ate brown rice and parsnips, possibly a turnip, and little else. At supper we learned that Mark had been keeping to this diet for weeks before we had arrived.

Next morning, when we could see him in the cruel light of day, Catherine and I decided that he was dying. We told him that we thought he was ill.

'It's only the poison coming out,' he said furiously. I rather think he meant it in a metaphysical context but we took it literally.

'Quite,' we said to each other. 'What shall we do?' We thought about it and decided to telephone the wisest person we knew, Christopher Gibbs, and set out for the village telephone clutching Mars Bars and fags. Christopher was rather amused when we told him we thought Mark was dying.

'Tell him to go and see Dr Latto,' he said. 'That's all he needs. Do stop worrying about him dying. Nonsense. You girls!' Dr Latto was a famous homoeopathic doctor. We crept back rather deflated.

As the weather improved, we began to feel that we had been in Mick's yard for ever and the urge to travel reasserted itself. One fine morning we set out in the direction of Hungerford. On the way our procession of people, horses, carts and dogs was split up by cars and lorries interspersing themselves. I turned around at one moment and saw Clancy, my boyfriend, driving a small cart careering downhill at full tilt. He was standing up, his raspberry-coloured velvet hat squashed sideways on his head, spectacles on the end of his nose, making desperate efforts at control. Mark looked aghast and swore. And so we progressed into Hungerford.

It was market day and cars lined the streets on either side of the road. I was driving the dogcart we got in Port Eliot, a very wide affair which I was not used to. As we trotted smartly down the main road, I thought I heard the noise of grinding metal and shouts of 'Stop, stop'. I looked back and saw that I had opened up the side of someone's car, like a can of sardines, with the hub cap of the dogcart. Naturally, my first instinct was to trot on but decency prevailed and I stopped. I had no money and Mark had to settle up in the end for forty pounds. He was angry.

The most captivating thing about life on the road was the pace – the sound of iron hooves and wheels on the road, the gradual change of scenery, the surprise round the corner or at the top of a hill. The rate of progress, between four and ten miles an hour, was perfect and, seated up on a cart or wagon, you could see over the tops of hedges and hills to the distant countryside, purply-blue and hazy. Every few hours we would have to water the horses and, bucket in hand, I always received a friendly greeting at farmhouse and cottage. The fiercest thing was always the ubiquitous resident sheepdog, which, upon seeing us – and particularly the lurchers – would rush out, a black-and-white streak of barking animal and showy aggression.

Nobody was ever unpleasant to us in our travels – they may have been surprised, but we were never turned away. We would camp on a lay-by if it were big enough to graze the horses, and sometimes a local farmer would let us into a field. Somehow our timing was nearly always wrong. It would be getting dark and we had found nowhere to stop, it would be raining and we had no firewood. I always had to put up my tent in the dark, slithering about and tripping over guy ropes and losing my tent pegs. But thanks to a mixture of Mark's innate common sense, daring, pertinacity and soul, we were never, finally, at a loss. We made little jokes about 'our leader', but without Mark this journey would never have taken place.

Our evening meal was a particularly nice time. Penny had assumed the mantle of practicality (thank God), and had taken over the shopping, cooking and washing-up. When I was there I was her obedient dogsbody, trailing along behind her and being helpful. She is a very good cook and learned how to manage our macro-cuisine on an open fire with great skill. She even invented a way to make apple-and-blackberry crumble on the fire in an old biscuit tin. Thrilling. We would sit around the glowing embers, drink dandelion coffee, smoke hashish, sing, gossip. The dogs would lie within the circle and we could hear the quiet clinking of the horses' tethering chains as they moved about cropping the grass.

One sunny summer afternoon Mark and I were travelling near Frome. Mark was reading the Ordnance Survey map, as he always did. He looked up and pointed down a steep little lane and said, 'Shall we try down there? Do you think we'll make it?' We didn't have any brakes on the wagon, because at this time Mark believed brakes were unnatural, but I nodded and said, 'Yes, we'll make it, all right.' We turned down the hill and after a few laboured paces Rizla sat down on her rump and we plummeted downhill, with an enormous noise like creaking thunder. After thirty yards and amidst bright sparks from her hooves we slid neatly into a ditch and then a hedge. Nothing and nobody was hurt and when we had finished laughing and soothing Rizla, who was rather surprised, we realized we were in a quandary and, like Pooh, could move neither forward nor backward. We were rescued by a jovial farmer, who hitched up his tractor to the wagon and towed it up to the top of the hill.

We saw no other travellers on the roads in the south of England but when we reached the Midlands, near Retford we suddenly saw ahead of us the familiar shape of a barrel-top wagon on the road. At last, real travellers. Mark could do a deal. The deal took the best part of two days. I watched the group of men sitting on the brow of a small rise in a field, arguing, gesticulating, shouting and muttering. The meeting went on and on when suddenly there was a spirited slapping of hands, cries of 'Good luck', and the deal was done.

Sometimes we were fortunate and passed by the houses of friends and would accept what we interpreted as pressing invitations to drop in. Since the houses were often beautiful and had great parks and yards and water, we tended to stay for a bit. We were passing near Wiseton and thought it would be nice to visit the Laycocks, nice to have a rest too: my aunt Jo lived near by and, strangely, was on the road, waving. Joe Laycock and his younger brother Ben were at home. Some of Ben's friends were also there. Dorothy, a fierce lady who had looked after things for years and was reputed to be a witch, looked at our ragged cavalcade, somewhat amused and somewhat cynical. Ben showed us where to go and we soon settled in.

There was an old racecourse at Wiseton and one afternoon I took Rizla down to it and galloped round as fast as she could go. It was like riding a medieval war horse in a jousting tournament.

The weather was wonderful that summer at Wiseton. One morning at breakfast someone said, 'Let's have a summer trip,' and we all fell on our Sunshine Yellow tablets and swallowed them. Penny said, 'The baked beans have just jumped off the plate,' and we went for a long walk through fairyland. Later on we were sitting round the fire when Joe strolled up.

'We're all tripping,' we chorused.

Joe looked amused. 'I wonder if you can peel this clove of garlic?'

He handed me a piece of garlic, which I unsuccessfully

attempted to peel. It looked and felt as if it had hundreds of layers of skin. None of us could do it.

Joe looked even more amused. 'I think you'd get more of a lift from my aeroplane than you'd get from drugs, even cocaine,' he said.

He had an old Tiger Moth, the real thing, just like Biggles, and the thought of him flying it was irresistible. He was very, very good-looking, with dark hair and wonderful blue eyes. Catherine looked interested and said she'd love to go for a spin, and I said that I would too. It was Catherine's turn first, and I watched utterly horrified as they zoomed about in the air, looping the loop and looping the loop backwards and stalling the engine and generally doing very frightening things. When it came to my turn, I managed to mutter that I couldn't be nearly as brave as Catherine and could we just go for a quiet spin, not too high as I didn't like heights. As we sailed over the country just above the trees, and so low that I could see the birds in the hedges, I felt serene and peaceful and was not frightened at all. Years later Joe's sister Martha told me that this was the most dangerous thing you could do and that it was called 'hedge hopping'!

Chapter Sixteen

I walked into the chemist's in Launceston to buy some Nuits St Georges. The chemist went downstairs to the cellar to fetch it and I was left alone. On the counter I suddenly noticed an extremely large tin of my favourite drug, drinamyl, also known as purple hearts. I couldn't believe my luck and quickly emptied hundreds of pills into my basket and covered them with a scarf.

I deliberated. Should I leave right now, or should I wait like an innocent person and go through with my purchases in the normal way? I decided to act innocent and then if he noticed the loss of the tablets he'd know it couldn't have been me. I emerged into Launceston high street in a glow of triumph and picked up a biker on a Harley-Davidson that I spied in the square. His name was Jim and we roared around the north Cornish lanes and to Dozmary pool on Bodmin Moor, fortified by purple hearts and hashish, his contribution. Mark was at Glastonbury and we biked up there to see him. When we got there, I urged Jim to bike up the Tor, which is steep but has a small spiral path running up to the top. Halfway up Jim got unaccountably nervous. 'I don't like it here,' he growled and the Harley began to behave like a nervous horse, bucking and shying on the path. 'Go on, go on,' I yelled and on we went through low menacing clouds and driving rain. Mark and Jim got on quite well and Mark told us to go north to Shropshire which was as far as the cavalcade had got.

We sped northward like hell's angels and, taking a cross-country route, we arrived at a nice-looking pub, outside which were two wagons, two coloured horses, some dogs and Penny Cuthbertson and Angus Wood. After a couple of days, mostly spent getting to know the landlord, the purple hearts were finished and Jim departed. Penny had gone some-where for the weekend and Angus and I were left alone. Angus, who was a stalwart character, was known as the Colonel by his friends and he was adorable. He had his own wagon and a horse called Jacob, who was sold as a gelding but turned out to be a 'rig' (one ball), which caused great complications for the mares at certain times. Gus always took responsibility for himself, had his own maps and ideas of where and how to go. He and Mark always consulted on the route and Gus liked his own pace and would sometimes take off at a fast trot and disappear in a cloud of dust. He also had a very nice little rough-haired terrier called Geordie.

Gus and I were good friends and made each other laugh a lot. We had a few drinks and a quiet supper by the fire. I was exhausted. I had revved up my system into top gear for three weeks or so and now the drinamyl was finished I felt as if I had been beaten by metal rods. Thank goodness Penny had lent me her cosy, comfortable wagon for the weekend. I walked over the dewy grass, breathing the sweet fresh air, lit a candle, undressed and sank into bed and fell asleep.

I awoke slowly into what appeared to be a sea of blue flame. Clouds of smoke wreathed the wagon. I felt completely soporific and settled myself more comfortably. How pretty it was. Then I realized I was well and truly on fire. I really had to fight hard to get up. I had to force myself out of bed and over to the door, down the steps and outside, shouting Angus's name desperately. He came hurrying along.

'What's the matter, what's the matter? Oh my God!' We gazed at the now spectacular wagon. It looked like a red dragon belching fire and smoke. Gus rushed into action. 'I'll beat it out, you get the water.' After a bit we won the battle.

The next morning I stood forlornly and tearfully on the wet floorboards of Penny's wagon, surveying the damage. Her lovely afghan blankets were ruined, a little picture of a jockey was half burned, the paintwork was blackened. Shreds of burned material drifted in the air and there was a terrible, acrid stench. I couldn't bear it. Poor Penny. What a clumsy, selfish fool I was.

'Gussie, I've got to do something about this terrible mess. Please could we go to market and I'll get some new things. If not, Penny will kill me or I'll kill myself. Its just too ghastly and awful. I'll never forgive myself. Nobody will. Oh dear, oh dear.' We went to market and I got some replacements, not nearly as nice. When Penny came back, she behaved with great heroism. She was furious but she forgave me, though the subject was mentioned a fair bit.

I went back to London and sold my flat. I was convinced that I would never want to live in London again and that nobody would ever need money again. This was the direct result of taking so much acid and was a fantastic aberration, but at the time it seemed real enough.

Joshua and Caroline's boarding school, Frensham Heights, was reputed to be an enlightened school with a good scholastic and musical reputation for the children of rather unusual parents. They liked it and when I visited them I wasn't surprised. Lots of children ran in and out of the large, over-grown shrubbery, where they had built shelters and little houses. They smoked pot and giggled, and their existence seemed to be rather more *Lord of the Flies* than traditionally educational.

In the holidays we stayed with my friend Tats Bromley in Cadogan Gardens and went to a lot of discos in the evenings, where we would take Mandrax, drink and dance madly; fall over as our knees turned to cotton wool and laugh crazily while struggling to get up.

Chapter Seventeen

I heard on the grapevine that Mark and the cavalcade had reached the Welsh borders, near the county town of Montgomery, and that Mark had bought a farmhouse! I brooded and wondered and decided on a plan of action. I would ask Mark, very humbly, if I might come and live in his house. When I asked him the next time he came to London, he looked at me in a slightly puzzled way and said, 'Yes, of course you can.' Hooray!

Penny came to Cadogan Gardens to fetch me. We set off in my black Morris Minor car, which was stuffed full with all my belongings and my dog Leaf and we took off for the borders.

Penny said, 'It's nice to have another girl. There are so many awful boys there.'

'Oh?' I said. 'Who?'

'Well, Mark, Derek Fitzgerald, Kelvin Webb and Angus Wood.'

'Goody,' I said. 'They're all nice.'

Mark's house was called the Grove and lay about two miles outside Montgomery, a very pretty little town with Tudor and Georgian houses and a spacious main square. Dominated by the ruins of the castle above on a jagged spur, its centre was for me the Dragon, a large pub and one-time hotel. It was run by an old-fashioned and genial 'mine host' sort of man and his less expansive wife, Mr and Mrs Proe.

The Grove was a friendly smallholder's house built around the turn of the century out of red brick. It had a yard and a garden, a few acres of land, a hill covered in aggressive yellow gorse. It supported horses and one summer we grew a crop of hay and harvested it, by hand, and made an old-fashioned hay rick that looked like a Samuel Palmer painting.

In order to maintain his independence Angus had positioned his wagon in the orchard. After supper every night he and Geordie stomped off together and went to bed. One night while we were having supper we kept hearing a sort of crackling and roaring noise. It was autumn and, thinking it was a seasonal gale, we continued eating, but after a while the roaring had become louder and the sky had turned an ominous red. We threw down our forks and rushed outside as one body. Angus's wagon was ablaze, the flames furiously whipped by the wind. We did our best to put it out, but there wasn't much left, although next morning he found his passport, mysteriously intact and uncharred among a heap of ashes.

Apart from running water and electricity, the Grove was unmodernized and there was no inside lavatory. At a sale of farm implements Angus found an oddity. It was an outside family lavatory, a long bench with three holes carved in it. He set it up and dug a deep trench. Whenever we used it, we would throw in a spadeful of earth after our visit. But we were never uninhibited enough to visit it in threes.

We had lots of dogs, a greyhound and some lurchers, and among them there was a vile old bitch called Gretel, known as the Crocodile. One morning, as she was lying in the yard, Geordie must have gone too close to her and, with a ferocious snap of her jaws, Gretel killed him. I rushed out to find Angus and met him in the orchard with tears pouring down his cheeks, carrying a little wooden cross which he had bound with twine. He was looking for a tranquil place to bury Geordie. He was a lovely man, brave and straightforward and full of tender feelings.

Every morning Penny would bring me a cup of tea at nine o'clock and we would start the day. First we would clean up the sitting-room, brushing the floor and shaking the mats outside, lighting the fire and then cooking breakfast. Mark was given a cup of tea in bed. He slept in what would have been the parlour, I suppose, among piles of leather harnesses. Our rooms were sacrosanct and we didn't wander casually in and out. There had been a plan to make a door and window in the wall of Mark's room overlooking the yard. The bricks had been removed but then the weather turned cold, so a large carpet was hung up over the gaps. It looked like an Arabian wall hanging. Monster came to stay one night and, idly handling the carpet, he pulled it aside to discover the gap. I've never seen such a surprised and amused-looking face.

Every Monday morning Penny and I would gather up the dirty washing, make a shopping list and drive into Welshpool. There was one big drawback to living in the manner we did and that was mud. Welsh border rain is persistent and produces acres and acres of mud. For a lot of the year we lived in wellingtons. The yard was muddy and the road. The fields were muddy and round the gates, where the horses gathered impatiently in the afternoon, awaiting the arrival of their hay, the ground was more like a bog than dry land. We were often mud-splodged and our wellingtons were caked in it. This made our arrival at the launderette conspicuous and we were often asked to remove our boots.

Our shopping included buying lots of sheep's heads for the dogs. These were very cheap. After they had been boiled up and distributed, in an attempt at tidiness the skulls would be thrown on to a great pile in a corner of the yard. I thought they looked very bizarre, like the evidence of some strange religion that we practised.

At lunchtime we took ourselves off to a café, where we had a couple of Welsh rarebits on toast with poached egg on top. They were the best rarebits I have ever tasted, golden brown, grilled and bubbling, with lightly poached fresh farm eggs atop.

Penny invented another first-class treat, a hot bath. One Monday we were feeling particularly muddy and miserably cold. We swept, as best we could, into the friendliest local hotel and said, 'May we have a bath, please?' We were delighted and amazed when they said, 'Yes, um, that will be twenty-five pence each.' That first bath in the Golden Lion was no less than ecstatic. To be totally immersed in hot water, to soap and wash the body, to shampoo, rinse and squeak clean the hair, to wallow in the water, was heavenly. To have a bath was divine.

We made friends and acquaintances around the place. We met them at markets, fairs and in pubs. Mark met lots of old farmers and bought and sold horses and dogs as usual. My favourite was a man called Joe Higgins. He was a farmer who had a nervous wife and a son called Eddy. He was interested in horses and home brewing. He made the most tasty and potent cider and wine and every year held a huge party in his magnificent, brick-paved barn.

That year we were among the hundred or so people who gathered in the evening. There was a large bar at one end of the barn and great barrels of cider and beer were racked up waiting to be drunk. A few tables and chairs were ranged around the sides. The Higginses had travelling blood and there was a lot of country-and-western music. People milled and danced and talked to each other and laughed and guffawed. They surveyed each other, saluted each other, made fun of each other and gossiped. They whirled about the floor in patterns of colour and gradually moved towards the centre of the room. I thought that this was a sort of natural progression, until someone pointed out to me that it was inevitable because the floor sloped very gradually towards a drain in the middle. It was made like this in order to facilitate mucking out and sluicing with water.

I circulated, happily drinking Joe's nectar and talking to friends and acquaintances. I chatted to a debonair man called Tricky Dicky Davies, a star at the local trotting races, and made my way to the kitchen where I found a bottle of Mrs Higgins's sleeping pills. I swallowed two of them for good measure and had some more twelve-year-old cider. When I got back to the jollity in the barn, Joe presented himself and asked me to dance. He was a big man and wore heavy, old-fashioned working clogs. We set off to the strains of a waltz in a stately enough manner, but, very gradually, on the downhill gradient, we worked up some speed. Soon we were twirling like sun-crazed dragonflies, and before long we were completely out of control, spinning in ever decreasing circles towards our doom in the centre. We crashed heavily into the drain, our arms and legs entwined, and with Joe's clog painfully jammed on to the toe of my fragile silver boot.

Mark sold Joe his grey Arab stallion, Sagittarius, and another bond was forged. Joe bred a lot of foals by Sagittarius.

One grey, drizzly morning, when Mark and I were out riding, he said, 'I've found the most marvellous little house for you.'

'Oh?'

'Yes, it's lovely.'

'Where is it?'

'Quite near here, about a mile away. Just down the lane from Kelvin at Tan-ty-Nellon. I can't find out who owns it. I've asked everyone and nobody seems to know. I think that you could just move in.'

'Oh. Can we go and see it, then?'

'Um, yes, all right.'

The way was straight over the crossroads at the top of the lane which led to the Grove and up an even narrower lane opposite. Up on a hill on the right was an old farmhouse that Kelvin had bought a few months before. Then the lane turned into a grass track and narrowed still more. On the left was an inspiring view of the hills and valleys of the Welsh borders and on the right, just as we were going down a little dip to a stream, stood the Den. It was a two-storied, long and low stone-built cottage, looking out over the little stream, which splashed, gurgled and tinkled along through a surprisingly grand, three-arched Georgian bridge. A path led up to the back door, which was flanked by two huge yew trees. The setting and the building had a strange Japanese feel to it.

We opened the back door and stepped into a stone-flagged kitchen, proper big flagstones, not rubbish. Then into a sitting-room with an enormous fireplace, the swinging iron arm for the kettle still in place. The front door, which opened on to this room, didn't really shut properly and all day let in the singing of the stream and the rays of the sun. The wooden staircase, which was crumbling in some places, led upstairs to two raftered bedrooms. Most of the windows were broken, but in those days fresh air was one of my best friends. I fell in love with the Den on the spot and turned gratefully to Mark to thank him.

I went to a local auction with Penny and bought a carpet, a sofa, some chairs and a table, stuff for the kitchen and various sundries – all for eleven pounds. Jane Rainey gave me a double bed which she had bought for six pounds and I moved in. I walked to the Den from the Grove carrying a dustpan and brush and, accompanied by Leaf, proudly entered my new home. The first thing I did was to go out into the surrounding fields and collect firewood. I lit a fire and made a cup of tea. The kettle hummed in a satisfactory kind of way.

Every morning I was woken up by the splash of sunlight on my bedroom wall and the plashing of the stream. My nearest neighbour was Kelvin but I didn't see him very often. He lived in some seclusion with his girlfriend, Rose. I spent every day doing small household tasks, but in the evening I would get lonely and walk to the Grove for supper. The walk back was often illuminated by the moonlight, which turned the little grassy track into a silver ribbon. Every night an owl hooted from one of the yew trees and I could hear the sheep calling to each other and the soft tearing noise of their feeding.

On my fortieth birthday I was given two birthday cakes. One was black, chocolate, round and covered in Smarties. The other was white, square, classic, and dressed with pale blue rosettes. I am a Gemini, so it seemed appropriate. Mark came to collect me in the afternoon. I was waiting in my best dress – an Ossie Clark flowered silk affair of great beauty – when I heard the muffled thudding of hooves as Mark swept into view. He was driving a flat cart and looked very dashing. 'Happy birthday,' he called. 'Up you get.' We went up the track a bit in order to turn round. The view over the green sparkling valleys to the distant blue hills was breath-taking. We thought the track must have been an old drovers' road, and perhaps before that a Roman road, moving legions up and down the Welsh borders. When we arrived at the Grove, I found all my friends in the garden sitting on rugs and cushions around a fantastic spread dominated by these two wonderful birthday cakes. The black cake had been made by Penny and the white one by a neighbour called Lesley who had been a baker. Jane Rainey and her brother Julian Ormsby Gore had come from Shropshire. They gave me a silk handkerchief with the word 'Victory' emblazoned on it, which I thought appropriate for forty.

After tea we went to the pub at Llandyssil and celebrated with many drinks. I had moved into the Newcastle Brown stage of my life. My life has been marked by a taste for the strongest drinks appropriate to my locality. In some periods it has been gin and tonic, in others whisky, barley wine, Worthington E or Special Brew.

Much later I started to walk back to the Den. It was a most

beautiful early summer night. There was a full moon and, as I walked down the silver path, I reflected on my good fortune. Eventually, believing myself to have reached home, I turned right, and stepped into space. It seemed an age before I landed. I felt rather like Alice falling down the rabbit hole, down and down and down. I landed with a loud splash in the middle of the stream. I had walked past the Den into the centre of the bridge and stepped smartly off it. I was wet through but unhurt. I must have a guardian angel.

Sometime later, in the following spring, we went to a fair and left all the dogs locked up in one of Kelvin's stables. When we got back, we found to our horror that they had battered the door down and escaped and killed a sheep and three lambs. What a black night that was. In the morning Mr Davies, whose sheep they were, came round with a very grave face. He said that if I had my dog, Leaf, put down, he would say no more about it. What a kind and forbearing man. I had to agree and, with a heart as heavy as lead, I set off with Mark to visit the vet, a jovial man called Terry Boundy. We buried Leaf at the Den and planted his grave with primroses.

One evening when I was visiting the Grove, Mark and Kelvin and I got very stoned as we sat and chatted. Mark had a brilliant idea. 'Let's shave Hen's head,' he suggested to Kelvin.

'Oh no you jolly well don't,' I protested and so on.

'She'd make a jolly good Martian.'

'Yes. Or we could have her as a sort of religious icon, a kind of sub-Buddha,' they sniggered.

Of course in the end they wore me down and I was shaved and lathered and shaved, and lathered and shaved again. By then I didn't care. I woke up the next morning at the Den to find Penny stroking the top of my head and crooning, 'Poor Hen, oh poor Hen.' Alarmed, I sprang out of bed and looked in the mirror. I saw a complete stranger staring back. The image of an intense, rather worried middle-aged Mongolian monk confronted me. The top of his head was a ghastly grave-like green, where the sun and air had never penetrated. I gave a shriek, rushed out and flung myself on to Bonny, the mare that Mark had lent me. As I rode up the lane, I saw, to my horror and confusion, Mr Davies approaching me on his tractor. I quickly ran through a few introductions. Good morning, Mr Davies, you may not recognize me but . . . Good morning Mr Davies, it's Henrietta, funnily enough . . . As he grew near me, he let out a hearty bellow with a completely straight face. 'Good morning, Henrietta. How are you today?' A few days later, when we were in Welshpool cattle market, I heard that Mark had tried to put me in the ring as a 'creature from outer space'.

I quickly grew accustomed to my new look and the top of my head grew tanned and lost its green tinge, but I had to go to London and there I was greeted on all sides, up and down the King's Road, by incredibly rude remarks and comments.

Caroline and Joshua came to stay for the summer holidays and brought some schoolfriends with them. The Den hummed and echoed to their shouts and laughter. Joshua built a little wooden bridge across the stream and Caroline did the washing and hung up the clothes on bushes round the house. One day Caroline and I were riding into Montgomery to do some shopping. We went past Boundy the vet when I suddenly stopped, found the key to the surgery, rushed in and stole a box of pethidine from the stores. I was hoping to find cocaine, but decided that pethidine, which is a euphoric opiate used in birth, would do. Later on, in the evening, I lined everyone I could find into a row and slammed a phial of pethidine into their buttocks. A feeling of great happiness overcame all of us and we wandered around saying and believing that we were in heaven.

Chapter Eighteen

Too soon Mark announced that he wanted to move on. He intended to sell the Grove and move to a house in Hay-on-Wye. A feeling of consternation tinged with resignation came over me. I felt so sad. It had been the first time I had felt that I truly belonged to a group and now it was breaking up. Penny was going to Ireland to stay with Desmond Guinness, Kelvin had sold Tan-ty-Nellon, and Angus was moving down the borders. Mark's house in Hay-on-Wye was called Cym-Rythen. He had bought it from Bob Ho and Suki Potier, a glamorous couple who had to leave England for Hong Kong in a bit of a hurry because of a misunderstanding with the police about drugs. Kelvin saw my apprehensive face and said kindly, 'Don't worry, I'm sure more people than ever will beat a path to your door.' I wasn't so sure.

The months wore on and I was feeling sad: it was so lonely and I didn't have a car or a horse or any money. I did have a new dog though, and she was a delightful companion. One day I was walking into Montgomery to do some shopping when Terry Boundy came out of his house and said that a black and white Welsh sheepdog bitch had been hanging around his house all day and he thought she had been abandoned. He said I needed a dog and I said that if she was still there when I came back from Montgomery I would take her. I dillied and dallied in the town, went to the pub for a drink, gossiped a little to people and rather hoped that when I returned she would have gone, but of course she hadn't. I bent down and caressed her ears and told her she was mine and she followed me back to the Den.

Later on that night I half shut her in the door as she hesitated at the entrance – I don't think she had ever been in a house before. She shot away and disappeared over the brow of the hill. She must have been badly treated in her former life. After a while I stood at the door and called her new name out into the night air. 'Den, Den, Den.' I saw her watching me from a small distance and eventually she came back to me, half wagging her tail and with the start of a grin on her face. I introduced her to the stairs and we went up to bed.

I remember one day in December it was cold and I had collected a lot of wood and had a lovely big fire burning away. It was the middle of the afternoon and the light was just beginning to fade. I had an urgent wish to bathe, to be as clean as possible. I gathered up my towel and soap and flannel and went down to the stream which was in full spate. I undressed, stepped in and soaped myself all over. It was very cold but invigorating and pleasant. I stood in the rushing water and looked at the candlelit cottage windows and the kind trees surrounding it. Everything was so beautiful and suddenly it began to snow. Large, soft, warm flakes settled on my naked body. Den sat on my towel full of attention and concern. I felt really happy.

Of course, like everything else in life, as I have found, it didn't last. I decided to try and get a job. I was rather out of practice for that sort of thing, a bit old and without much experience. I decided to give the second-hand book empire at Hay-on-Wye a chance and set off in that direction. I saw Mark in London and told him what I intended to do. 'Well, you can't stay with me,' he said nervously. 'I've only just got away.' So I said that I'd stay with Kurt Shafhausser, who also lived just outside Hay.

Kurt was an American who had married a British girl called Maggie. They had led a lovely, merry Sixties life in London for a bit, but had decided to marry, move to the country and have children. When I got there, Kurt showed me his new addition to the house, a Tibetan 'gompa', a little temple. When he first came to England, Kurt had met a Tibetan monk, a high-up called Trungpa Rimpoche, and had been converted to Buddhism. He prayed many times a day and he also made his own elderflower champagne. He and Maggie lived in a very nice farmhouse on top of a hill, comfortable with bathrooms and a washing machine, about four miles from Hay. They owned a sheepdog called Nip, well named actually, and a corgi called Gelert, whom I adored and would play with for hours – he was a comic genius and had a great heart.

I telephoned Richard Booth, the bookshop impresario, and fixed up an interview with him.

'I've got a friend of yours staying with me,' he said.

'Who?'

'Marianne Faithfull.'

135

'Oh, good.'

Booth lives in Hay Castle, which is in the centre of the town. I decided it would be lucky to walk to Hay for my interview and I set off with Den the next morning. I arrived on time. Halfway through my interview Marianne came into the room and I thought that I had probably got the job. When he asked me what sort of salary I was thinking of, I said, 'Forty pounds a week.'

Marianne said, 'Hen!'

Booth swallowed and said, 'Just what I was thinking myself.'

We went to the Cinema, which is the largest shop in the Booth empire, and I met the newly appointed manager, William Bere, an ex-army man, and Michael Cottrell, who was the brains of the bookshop. He was an old-fashioned intellectual and really knew about second-hand books. He did all the catalogues and his tragedy was that he was going blind. He was very scathing about everyone, but thought I would be all right because he knew about Dom. I was not to live up to his expectations.

I told Booth that I had nowhere to live. He said I could have the top flat in the old spike which he had just bought. It was an excessively gloomy building, a Victorian workhouse in an H shape where men and women, including old married couples, had been separated upon entry. Cotters gave me a couple of posters, one of Thackeray and one of Swift, which I stuck up on the wall. Booth gave me some logs from the castle store, and my old friend Frank English, who had been putting up shelves for Richard, gave me his little iron bed.

My work was rather boring. It had nothing to do with selling books, which I like, but all to do with endlessly rearranging long rows in shelves in the Cinema. Booth bought books in huge container-loads which sometimes had to wait for ages in customs awaiting payment. He would go to San Francisco and buy six bookshops and ship them back to England. So when the containers did arrive, unloading them was the hardest work I had ever done. I had to be able to sort, price and shelve a book in one minute. It took me at least five minutes to start with, but I soon speeded up and memories of authors and books that I had long forgotten came flooding back. Sometimes I came across rare editions and my fingers learned to tingle when I picked them up. Bill Bere wanted everything in alphabetical order. Cotters despised this and exuded an air of sardonic disapproval whenever he found me on my knees fishing out a Dornford Yates from a row of Trollope.

Bill and I became drinking companions. Hay was a great drinking town, with even more pubs than second-hand book-shops, and Bill and I spent our lunchtime and our evenings in them. He had a wife in Wiltshire somewhere and I was on my own so it suited us. We did the *Telegraph* crossword puzzle every day and played bar billiards quite a lot. Hay was full of 'characters', and one of the most colourful was April Ashley, who had had one of the first sex changes and had been married to Bobby Corbett's brother for a bit and had a rather lurid divorce. She was a great favourite of Booth and he had created her a duchess. Booth had made a stab at independence for Hay, with himself as king, and had generously doled out a few titles here and there. I don't believe Hay ever succeeded in its bid for independence, but Richard was very keen and not to be deterred.

April and her friend Jane, with whom she lived, would

spend many evenings with us in the pubs having an uproarious time. I used to ask April about her operations and she obligingly would tell all. She did not hold back on the harrowing details and the pain she had experienced. She was a nice person, old April, camp and witty and very kind. She admired strength of character and balls, and had plenty of them herself.

Marianne and her friend Michelle spent quite a lot of time with Booth at the castle and would give nice little dinner parties, to which I would be asked, together with Kurt and Maggie and Frank English. Michael Cottrell was scandalized by the intellectual level of these gatherings and tut-tutted about the company Booth was keeping and prophesied doom in all directions. Frank was a terrible drunk and annoyed Booth very much by always drinking up and finishing every bottle in sight. I don't think that I was much better, but perhaps not quite so obvious.

Booth decided on the opening date for the spike as a bookshop. It was to be an American bookshop, specializing in the civil war and there was to be a huge opening party, to which the American ambassador would be asked. So at least a hundred thousand books had to be found and priced and shelved, all in about three weeks. A period of madness followed. Another man called Bill – Bill Ripley – was found to organize this, and he and I worked together. We didn't have too much idea of the general layout of the shop, so we had to invent it – novels, plays, poems, biographies, topography and so on. We were both exhausted, half mad, drunk. We began to dream books, piles of second-hand books lying about waiting to be sorted. Dusty books, tattered books, obscure books, esoteric books, Mark Twain, all clamouring for a place. I told Booth about these haunting dreams and he replied jauntily that it happened to everybody. One night just before the opening party, I dreamed that I was surrounded by a lot of old, sad people. They thronged round me and said, 'Henrietta, why haven't you asked us to your party?' I couldn't think of an answer and woke up. The next day, I was taking down a bit of wall in my little flat and I found a cheap metal chain and medallion of St Francis, buried and hidden in the mortar.

Bill Ripley and I were driven to making love in odd corners amidst spiders' webs and dust and falling plaster, as much to escape the books as from real sexual passion.

The great day arrived and the ambassador and the party seemed to go off all right. I saw Cotters eyeing our placement of books in a very deprecating way and we had indeed made some laughable mistakes.

The next day Booth gave me the sack. I was stunned. 'But I've never worked so hard,' I stuttered.

'I simply cannot afford you, Henrietta,' he said. And that was that.

Luckily, Marianne was up in arms and when she taxed Booth with it and he said, 'I can't think of anyone who would employ Henrietta,' she replied, smart as a whip, 'I will.'

The Sunday before I left Hay was Easter Sunday and I decided to go to eleven o'clock Communion. It was a beautiful morning and as I walked up the aisle I saw the familiar figure of our Poet Laureate, Sir John Betjeman, sitting with the defrocked ex-Bishop of Southwell, who had dallied with a chorus girl. He had married David and Martha Mlinaric, and was also working for Booth. I nodded to them and after the service we went to a pub and drank lots of pink gins and made jokes at Richard Booth's expense.

Chapter Nineteen

Life with Marianne, in a mews flat in St John's Wood, was fairly desultory to start with. She had no money and was waiting to go on tour in Ireland. Her tiny little flat, which belonged to a friend of her mother, was behind the beautiful white Regency houses looking out over the park and Queen Mary's rose garden. Her doctor, who oddly enough was the brother of the saintly homoeopath Dr Latto, had a practice in Harley Street and for some reason was extremely generous in handing out prescriptions for amphetamines and Mandrax. I used to go to him once a week to keep myself together and fell in with a group of ne'er-do-wells whom I met in the chemist's. We used to go 'brickering' together, browsing through skips and empty houses, finding all sorts of good things. 'Brickering' is a highly enjoyable sport when charged up on amphetamines.

Marianne's tour was scheduled for early summer, and one morning, she, her boyfriend Colin and I got on an Aer Lingus plane and flew to Dublin. The record company in Ireland which was to look after us was called Hawk Records but known as the Murphia, tough nuts obviously just in it for the money. My job was that of a minder and minding Marianne turned out to be all-consuming.

The tour took us all over Ireland and sometimes involved hours and hours of driving, with stops at Little Chefs and hurried, greasy meals and snacks. I had never been on this sort of road and I found it absolutely exhausting, and the Murphia and I disliked each other with some passion. I loathed them because they were totally philistine and condescending; they hated me because I knew nothing about touring and I was English.

I liked gigs, though. I liked it when we actually arrived and were all set up and the gig started. Marianne is very popular in Ireland, everybody loves her. They think of her as a cross between a convent girl and a witch. When her small blonde figure appeared on stage, a roar of tumultuous applause would go up and we would be away.

The very first gig she did started shakily. For a moment I thought that it would be a disaster. It was in a huge venue known as the Snake Pit in Dublin, a vast auditorium filled with shouting, gesticulating people. I peered through the stage curtains and was exceedingly glad that it wasn't me who had to go on. Marianne and I stood in the wings waiting for her cue. As it came up, she turned to me and said, 'I can't go on.' As she spoke, she was sick all over me. I seized her by the shoulders, spun her round to face the stage and firmly booted her on. She arrived centre stage at a half-run and with her arm raised in a Nazi salute, trying to keep her balance. It went down very well with the audience. She sang rather flat but they didn't mind at all.

Things improved after this. Marianne stopped being so nervous and we played in some nice places. My time was spent looking after Marianne, taking her clothes to the cleaners, waking her up in the morning, seeing she was ready to leave at the right moment. I enjoyed it, I've always loved her, although I've been exasperated by her too, and I certainly earned my money.

Chapter Twenty

Marianne went to America. Her record company, Island records, wanted her there and I stayed behind in the mews flat. It was a strange time. I had no money and no job, but I did have amphetamines and any drink I could get hold of. I was very isolated and took to stealing the groceries that the milk-man left outside the front doors of people in the mews. Nobody ever seemed to notice.

I had an old boyfriend called Charlie Blackwell, a barman from the Star pub in Shrewsbury. He arrived on the doorstep one day and I, rather reluctantly, let him in. He was obsessively in love with me and so I, in turn, was rather bored with him. Anyway there he was, with a large wad of money in his pocket and dying to go to the pub. After a couple of days I was thoroughly fed up with being told how marvellous I was and how much he loved me. I was even fed up with drinking in the pub – anything I wanted and as much of it as I could take. They loved him there – no wonder – and this only added to my mounting boredom and near fury.

On the afternoon of the third day I left the pub early and went home. I double-locked the door and sat by the window waiting for the inevitable arrival of a drunken, bleating, boring Charlie. He tried the door, it wouldn't open.

'You must go home now,' I said, out of the open window. 'Back to Shrewsbury.'

'No, no, I must talk to you. I love you so much, more than anything in the world.'

'Go away, Charlie, there's nothing to say.'

Instead of going, he bent down and picked up a wire coat-hanger which was lying in the gutter, twisted it around a bit, inserted it into the keyhole and to my astonishment and fury opened the door.

I met him halfway up the narrow mews staircase. Rage had taken me over. I was blind with anger, I could see only through a red haze. I raised my leg and kicked him in the middle of his chest as hard as I could. His body was lifted into the air and he somersaulted down the stairs to crash into the little hallway. I stared at him. His body looked odd. I ran down the stairs and tried to listen to his breathing. I couldn't hear it. I tried to find his heartbeat. I couldn't. I rushed to find a mirror and held it to his lips. It didn't cloud over. My God, I'd killed him. Oh my God, what do you do when you've killed someone?

I thought of Catherine Tennant. She might know what to do. 'Catherine, hello. I know this sounds stupid, but I think I've just killed someone. I kicked him downstairs and he's not breathing and I don't know what to do.'

Catherine was admirably cool. 'You must ring up the police and your solicitor,' she said. 'Probably in that order.'

'Well, I'll go and check first, make quite sure, oh my God.'

I checked and still found no breathing and no heartbeat. I stood there looking intently at Charlie and I was suddenly filled with the same murderous rage as I had been before. Bloody man, I hadn't wanted him there in the first place. I stared and stared at him, rage swiftly taking over my mind again. I raised my foot and kicked him, as hard as I could, right under his heart. Slowly, Charlie sat up.

'Now will you damned well go,' I said.

Around Christmas time I decided to go and stay for a bit with my old friend John Michell, the antiquarian. He had a house in Bath, 11 Miles Buildings – he always seemed to live at a number 11 somewhere or other. When I arrived he made me welcome and then said that he was going to spend a couple of days with his brother. 'If you could bind a few of these pamphlets for me while I am away,' he said, 'I should never forget it.' He waved towards a table, on which lay a pile of papers. I picked one up. It was entitled, 'Jesus Christ, the great cock.' It was nicely printed and the cover was red, black and gold. It had some illustrations of a man in a huge great turban, which made me think that perhaps there was a phallic context to the whole thing. There were some red silk and bodkins lying on the table and John showed me how to make five holes in the spine and how to sew it. It was my first lesson in book-binding.

John left and I passed my time taking Den for long walks on the tow-path by the canal and binding 'Jesus Christ'. I hoovered the whole house and did some dusting and hoped that John wouldn't be too angry when he got back. Joshua was living with his girlfriend Susan quite near by and I saw them from time to time. Joshua had won the football pools the year before – not a huge amount but nice to have – and was roaring around on a powerful motorcycle. By the time John came back I had finished all the binding and there was a neat and beautiful pile of books. He was very pleased.

One morning, just after I had woken up, I heard a voice in my head say, 'Go to Ireland.' I wondered long and hard about this and decided that it might have been St Patrick and that I had better do it. John said that I should ask Susan for the air fare. She was quite rich and so I did. I thought I would go and stay with Penny and Desmond at Leixlip Castle and see what happened. Susan gave me a sort of flying kennel for Den and one morning she and Joshua drove me to Bristol Airport and we flew off to Dublin.

I telephoned Leixlip. 'Can I come and stay?' I said.

'Hen, how lovely. Of course you can. When?'

'Well, I'm at Dublin airport actually.'

There was a pause.

Help, I thought, what have I done? I don't know Desmond at all well.

Penny's voice came on the telephone. 'Hen, you had better take a taxi to Leixlip.'

I arrived somewhat nervous and, having shouted a bit, let myself in through a side door. I met Desmond and Penny in the hall. We said hello and they told me that they had to go off to the theatre. Suddenly Desmond's voice rose to a roar of rage. 'Get that dog out of here!'

I looked over the hall and saw Den having a shit on a priceless Aubusson rug. Poor Den, confused by her flight, the wait in the airport and her very whereabouts, was committing a cardinal sin. It was awkward for me too. Not a particularly good start, I thought.

After a couple of days Penny had to go to England. She said, 'Hen, Desmond likes a bit of time to himself when I'm away so you can't stay here. But you can go to Roundwood if you like.'

Chapter Twenty-One

Roundwood was an eighteenth-century Irish Georgian house owned by the Irish Georgian Society, of which Desmond was the president. Originally it had belonged to a family called Hamilton, who had become more and more broke, in the way of Ascendancy families, and had been forced to sell. Luckily, the IGS was able to buy it with the help of an American benefactor and had restored it to its former glory. The man mainly responsible for this was a dedicated member of the Society and his name was Brian Molloy. I was to meet him in a bar called Murphy's in the square of Mountrath, the nearest town.

Roundwood was sixty miles from Leixlip and lay in County Laoise, which I had never even heard of. When I asked Desmond where it was, he replied, 'It is the Massif Central of Ireland, my dear.' So I was none the wiser.

It was a Saturday morning and when I got off the bus in Mountrath the first thing I did was buy a pair of wellingtons for four pounds as I thought Roundwood life might encompass these. Then I went to Murphy's. There was a small man in the bar, whom I correctly took to be Mr Murphy. He looked up and said, 'Good evening.'

Not realizing that this was the standard Irish greeting any time after midday, I replied, 'Good afternoon. I've come here to meet Brian Molloy. Have you seen him?'

'I have not,' he said, 'but if he said he'd be here, he will.'

I settled down with a glass of Guinness, and ten minutes later Brian walked in. He looked about thirty and had slightly balding hair and large, liquid, bird-like eyes. He was smallish and looked somehow like a very intelligent priest. I took to him immediately. After a while we went and bought a chicken and some butter in the country market and set out for Round-wood. Brian had a small terrier called Dilly, who trotted everywhere at his heels. We drove for a few miles and some mountains loomed up. 'What are they?' I asked. 'The Slieve Bloom mountains,' Brian said. Oh yes, I thought, of course, the Massif Central. 'They are full of the boys on the run,' he said. 'We're only ten miles from Portlaoise, after all.' Oh, I thought, he means the IRA.

We turned through some rather battered iron gates into an avenue of lime trees and proceeded slowly up a potholed drive. Brian stopped the car and we let the dogs out. We cleared a bend and there sat Roundwood, a darling mid-eighteenth-century building, looking for all the world like a gigantic doll's house. 'Oh,' I said. 'Isn't it lovely?'

There were three stone steps up to the front doors which opened directly into the hall. It was panelled and painted white and was two stories high, with two enormous windows facing each other across its length. The stairs went up to a small landing facing one of the windows and then swept round into a gallery with arresting Chinese Chippendale carving, like a musicians' gallery where you could stand and look down into the auditorium of the well-polished, wooden-floored hall. It was a beautiful and novel arrangement, and one which never failed to give me pleasure. On one side of the hall there was a small morning room which looked out over the lawn, and a large drawing-room. On the other lay the dining-room which led through a mysterious little passage to the kitchen, the cellar and the back door. This opened out on to a beautifully cobbled yard, and beyond were stables, outhouses and various unused buildings. In the middle of the yard, there was a well, though it was not used any longer. I felt absolutely at home.

'You can choose which bedroom you would like,' Brian said, so I went slowly up the staircase to the first floor and opened all the doors. One room was obviously his, so I shut the door. The next room was bright green and had an adjoining bathroom; it looked two ways, over the park at the front of the house and the lawn at the side. The room opposite also looked over the park; it was Chinese-yellow and had a bathroom. The fourth room was grey and looked out over the yard. I chose the green room and unpacked my things and showed Den her new place.

The floor above had obviously once been the nursery floor and still had faint echoes of childish things. It had a large landing and four rooms opened off it. I half expected a rocking horse to be standing there and the sound of children's laughter.

Brian had a great gift for life, so that every moment of being with him was a pleasure. I found he had a classical Irish sense of irony and humour, irreverence and wit. When I came downstairs, we went for a walk with the dogs. He showed me the great barn and a path that encompassed the land that used to belong to Roundwood. I felt very easy with him, as if I had known him for a long, long time.

We had dinner that night in the drawing-room on a small round table in front of a roaring beech-log fire. Country market chicken, roasted to perfection, spuds, some vegetables and a filthy red wine bought from Mr Murphy. All his wine was filthy, like the reprehensible Algerian stuff we bought in the Fifties. Nevertheless, it didn't stop us drinking it.

Brian had an almost theatrical ability to conjure up a dinner which was always excellent and to produce a setting in the space of an hour and somehow give it a feeling of both originality and permanence. He was a very good and quick cook who made absolutely no fuss over the preparation. The one place we never ate in was the kitchen, I think he rather despised kitchens. His life style, though eccentric, had a certain formality, so I always had a bath before dinner and changed into my beloved afghan robe.

Brian told me that he was expecting a teenage boy called Patrick Coynyngham to arrive on Monday evening. He was reputed to be a bit of a handful and his mother thought he needed some direction in life. Desmond thought he might find it at Roundwood.

On Monday a very tall, thin, bird-like creature with a huge beak appeared and shook hands with me. 'How long have you been here?' he inquired.

'Since Saturday,' I replied.

'Oh,' he said. 'I feel as if you've been here for years.'

Patrick and I settled down very quickly with Brian at Roundwood. Every morning we would drive to Roscrea, a town about fourteen miles away, and work on the restoration of another Irish Georgian house called Damer House. We were painting with rollers and trays, which is quite easy, but not if you are Patrick Coynyngham. Sometimes, unable to manoeuvre his roller, Patrick would get very frustrated and fling it on the ground and burst into tears and sit on the stairs crying and moaning. We took no notice of this whatsoever and it soon passed. Actually, it was pretty funny. Every lunchtime Patrick and I went to the pub and got a bit drunk. We would return to Damer House in a very jolly mood, but Brian said we behaved like a couple of tinkers!

Every evening we would do some shopping and go home to Roundwood. The fire, with those great beech logs, took only a second to get going and by the time I had had my bath and changed I could scent the delicious smells of dinner cooking. I would come downstairs to find a table set up in one room or another and occasionally in the formality of the dining-room.

We made a few expeditions and the most exciting was to Cork in the snow. Usually it never snows in Cork, but it started as Brian, Patrick, Den, Dilly and I set out. We spent the night in a small Georgian house, lived in by two ladies straight out of the pages of Jane Austen. They didn't want Den in the house, so I had to leave her outside and rescue her in the middle of the night. I got caught sneaking her out again in the morning and a certain *froideur* set in. We went to the castle and the sea at Kinsale. We visited endless houses, ruins and towers, and people connected with the IGS. We had delicious meals, a particularly good one in Hedli Anderson's restaurant in Kinsale, and we ended up in Myrtle Allen's hotel, Ballymaloe House.

I had often heard people talk about Ballymaloe and looked forward keenly to visiting it. It was enthralling, the only hotel

I have been to that was like staying with someone in their house in the country. Brian and Myrtle Allen were good friends, so this added to the illusion. The whole house is crammed full of paintings by Jack Yeats, brother of W.B. Ballymaloe has the largest collection in the world of this excellent painter and the canvases are hung close together so that they can really be seen.

Our rooms were adjoining, and Den was made welcome. We had drinks in the bar and a really good dinner, as good as I've ever had. It was a jolly evening with some sort of party going on and we stayed up late. The next morning, when I came down to breakfast at the big table in the dining-room, I found great jugs of fresh orange juice on the table. I thirstily drank two glasses and thought that it was the most civilized place in the world.

Chapter Twenty-Two

Desmond telephoned and said that Bob and Suki had telephoned from Hong Kong and wanted me to go and stay with them until Suki's baby was born. Suki apparently wanted a companion, an old friend to be with her during the day while Bob was at the office. I seemed to fit the bill and, though I was really happy at Roundwood, decided to go. After all, I had never been to the Far East.

Brian, Patrick and I had some really affectionate and rather sad evenings before I went. Brian said, 'We'll never do this again, it's been so nice.' I remembered Patrick's scrawled notes in the visitors' book, written when he was particularly emotional, but immediately forgotten. Things like: 'Sorry, I've been such a nuisance. Thank you for having me.' I giggled to myself and agreed.

'Can I come back again?' I asked Brian.

'Yes, of course,' he said. 'And I'll look after Den.'

Michael Rainey decided to come on my flight to Hong Kong. He sort of took over. He and Jane had a clothes business called Tropical Belt, and he wanted to check out the manufacturing end of things in Hong Kong. As I hadn't been anywhere in a long time, I was quite pleased. We decided that it was such a long flight, eighteen hours, that we would stop off in Sri Lanka for a couple of days.

We boarded the flight and it was like a cocktail party. We managed to drink solidly until we reached Colombo Airport, and staggered off the plane into a taxi. I had to pee and the driver stopped at a little house in a coconut grove. As I pulled the lavatory chain, the whole thing, tank and everything, collapsed on my head. Did I pull too hard, or was it just jerry-built?

Michael wanted to buy some sapphires – Colombo was apparently the place – and we met a strange jeweller, who was oddly touchy and yet possessive. We remembered our old friend Stas de Rola had a house on an island somewhere in the south and we decided to visit him. When we got on the train, it was with some amazement that we found the jeweller sitting in the adjoining seat to ours.

When we got to our destination, we went to a café by the sea and there was Stas, sitting at a table with a girl. 'Aha, the same cast, I see,' he said. 'What are you doing here?'

'We're on our way to Hong Kong to see Bob and Suki, and we've come to see you and your island.'

'Well, there it is, my dears,' and he flung out an arm and pointed at a small island about a quarter of a mile off the shore. 'There is an octagonal house on it built by a man called the Comte de Mornay, who got involved in a ghastly scandal at the Victorian court and fled here to spend the rest of his life in exile.'

'How do we get there?' I asked. 'Do you have a little boat?'

'We walk,' said Stas. 'At low tide, which it is now, we walk.' I gaped. 'There is a secret underwater sea path, known to very few,' said Stas, 'and I will show it to you.'

We entered the sea, Stas leading the way, and waded, further and further out. The water came past my ankles to my knees, then to my waist. I thought, Perhaps it's a joke.

But the water reached no further than my chest and, twisting and turning to follow Stas's progress, we eventually arrived on the white, sandy shore of the little island. What an enchanted place it proved to be, like Prospero's island. Encircling paths led gently upward and in various nooks and crannies marble seats looked out over the sparkling, blue sea. Statues of gods and nymphs gazed out to sea and a herd of small deer bounded past us.

We reached the summit effortlessly and there stood a mid-Victorian, octagonal house, a great surprise. We spent a wonderful day swimming and strolling round the enchanted island and caught the train back to Colombo the next morning.

Chapter Twenty-Three

The descent from the sky on to the tarmac at Kai-tak Airport is one of the most frightening experiences I have undergone. A tiny landing strip surrounded by mountains suddenly appeared and I realized that it was intended for our aeroplane. It looked impossible, far too small and short and narrow. Surely we would overrun the strip and crash into the mountains. I closed my eyes. We landed.

Bob and Suki were waiting at the airport with a huge car and a driver. As we drove through the thronged streets of the city, I thought I'd never seen so many people in my life before. There were thousands of them. There were street markets everywhere, selling everything. Huge skyscrapers were being built all around, with hundreds of figures swarming all over them. 'The scaffolding is made from bamboo poles,' Bob said. I felt oppressed by the volume of life in the streets and was glad when we left the town of Hong Kong behind and headed for the tiny village of Shek-O where Bob and Suki lived.

They lived in a little house with a beautiful garden right on the edge of the South China Sea, with a jetty sticking out into the water where a boat could tie up. A verandah ran right down the front of the house with sofas and chairs arranged on it. The South China Sea is the most amazing colour – every tint of jade from the darkest green to the palest and most opalescent. On it sail a multitude of little junk fishing boats, their sails glistening in the sun so that they look as if they are made from mother-of-pearl.

The thing that took me slightly aback was the precautions that had to be taken for practically everything. A twenty-five-foot-high wire fence ran right round the house, even cutting off the sea, and all the gates and doors were double-locked. Bob saw me looking and said with a faint smile, 'All this is because of my father. He's so rich that there's always a chance of my being kidnapped and held to ransom. They do that here, you know.'

Bob went to his father's office every morning. It had been pointed out to me on the drive from the airport – a sky-scraper in the shape of an immense Emmental cheese. He didn't get back till early evening and Suki and I had the day to ourselves. She had great cupboards full of clothes bought at the Paris sales and largely unworn. I found a loose black and yellow dress from somewhere, rather smart, and lived in it. We did very little: Suki was eight months pregnant and I found the heat overwhelming. The humidity was over ninety per cent and it was like living in a bowl of hot soup.

When Bob got back, he would smoke some joints made from heroin and cool out. It must have been hell for Suki, who couldn't smoke because of her pregnancy, but she never said so. We often had English food for dinner, shepherd's pie, fish pie, macaroni cheese, and it was strange to sit in Shek-O eating food from a past life.

We went to lunch in a hotel on the coast called the Peninsula and I got a whiff of far-off, more leisured colonial days. Great wooden fans hung from the ceiling, rotating slowly with dull clicks and thuds. There were enormous verandahs with rattan tables and chairs and comfortable sofas. There were wide passages and cool air and an impeccable staff dressed in spotless white. It felt very Somerset Maugham. We had oysters flown in from Sydney, Aberdeen Angus steaks flown in from Scotland, good French wine, delicious liqueurs . . . I began to feel very cheerful. 'It's the last place left that really has a feel of the British Empire about it,' said Bob.

One weekend we decided to go to Macao. I remembered reading somewhere that Macao was the wickedest city in the world, so I was terribly excited. Macao is on the Chinese mainland and still belongs to the Portuguese. Its purpose is gambling, an Eastern Monaco, and thousands of people of every class from Hong Kong hurry over to Macao every weekend to dice with fortune.

Bob's father, Stanley, owned all the transport to Macao, the Star ferry and the hydrofoils. We decided to go by Star ferry and return on the hydrofoil. The Star ferry ships are old and wooden with brass fittings and polished rails and pink, shaded lights. It takes several hours to cross in this way and there were snug, clean and inviting little cabins. It was the height of romance to me.

We arrived in Macao. It has an immense harbour, which is why the Portuguese chose it in the first place, but it is shallow, so that through the ages it has become less and less useful and now it is badly silted up. The green mainland of China spreading out beyond the city was an enticing vision. We took a cab to an astonishing huge round building swarming with doormen dressed in the uniform of the Swiss Papal Guard at the Vatican. I gaped.

'What on earth is all that?' I asked.

'That is where we are staying,' said Bob. 'My father owns it. Actually he owns all the gambling concessions in Macao as well.'

That night we visited all sorts of gambling establishments, from the extremely modest to the haunts of the international multi-millionaires. We travelled by rickshaw, sometimes pulled by a man, which inevitably made me feel guilty. The first place we went to was a little boat in the harbour, where people sat in a gallery above and let down their bets in small baskets. This was a very cheap game. We progressed up the financial ladder until after midnight we landed up at the roulette tables in our hotel, where several big American and Japanese players were operating. It was exciting for a while to watch these inscrutable faces leaning over the tables, dealing with vast sums of money, but after an hour or two I decided to go to my room and explore the nature of the room service.

We had two bodyguards to accompany us on this trip. Bob was wearing a pale pink linen suit, bought from Michael Rainey at Hung on You, and was an unnervingly conspicuous figure. I'm sure if someone had really wanted to pick him off, it would have been easy.

Another thing we used to do sometimes, which I liked very much, was to wander down to Shek-O village from the house and have a bowl of noodles in a little café or, in my case, a bottle of Guinness, export and ice-cold. The village seemed to be timeless, with people going about their business as they always had. There were lots of chow-like dogs wandering about and I wondered if we ever ate them. I had some snake soup once and it was delicious.

Soon it was the season of typhoons. I didn't know what a typhoon was until one suddenly descended on Shek-O and great palm trees and some rooftops were just whisked into the air and swept away. Suki started to have her baby in the middle of one and, since we were fourteen miles away from the hospital and the roads were said to be near impassable, I experienced some moments of pure panic. In the end, when the contractions seemed to be getting awfully close together, an ambulance appeared and she was carried out. I went with her. I had to crawl along the ground on my tummy to the ambulance, so as not to be swept away.

Suki's baby was born in the nursing home shortly afterwards. It was a little girl and very pretty, but the rejoicing was not the same as if it had been a boy. I had not quite realized that this was the feeling among the Chinese and I was a bit shocked. Apparently girls were not expected to go into business, and there was a whole empire waiting for this baby to take over. So it was on rather a subdued note that I left for England shortly after the birth.

Chapter Twenty-Four

I picked up my daughter Caroline in England and we flew
back to Ireland together. I was dying to get back to Roundwood. When we got there, Brian was out and Caroline and I
wandered around the beloved house and garden until he got
back. There were shouts and squeals and hugs and kisses. I
gave Brian a bauble I had picked up, we had dinner and I went
to bed with the familiar sound of the rooks outside my
bedroom window, squabbling and chattering and finally sett-
ling down amongst the rustle and sway of the beech tree
which was their home.

Soon a young renegade called Roderic O'Connor appeared.
He was the younger brother of my friend Nicholas Gormanston and he had a plan. He had heard in Dublin that the singer
Eric Burdon and his band, the New Animals, were looking for
a large, isolated country house to record an album in. They
had their own mobile recording studio (hired from the
Rolling Stones) and sound engineers, and they wanted peace
and quiet and beds and dinner. They were willing to pay

three hundred pounds a day, so it was a pretty irresistible offer.

Brian was dead against it and most apprehensive but couldn't resist the money. He decided to make himself scarce and went away, leaving Caroline and me, Roderic and his cook, a beautiful girl called Camilla, to look after everything.

The musicians arrived in dribs and drabs and gradually assembled. Eric arrived last, while we waited on tiptoe, and finally any notion of peace and quiet was dispelled entirely. They all drank like fish and naturally smoked hashish. The keyboard player was a very difficult man, a perfectionist and an idealist. They told me keyboard players were always tricky. The producer, Tony, and his girlfriend were an island of civilization amid the gossip, chaos and disorder, but it was the greatest fun and we all thrived on it.

A serious rift grew between the management and the artists. The management, who came and went, once found a joke newspaper that I had started, featuring them in a very sinister role. Things grew so bad that we hid the master tape in the false top of a wardrobe and when they arrived unexpectedly one day they couldn't find it.

We spent a lot of time in a pub in Mountrath called, appropriately somehow, El Paso. We went there at lunchtime and in the evenings and became great friends with the owners. We went to another pub up in the mountains called the Village Place. This was completely isolated and full of strange mountain men and wild figures. My favourite was an endearing and charming rascal called Sean Higgins, a great friend of Brian's who often came to Roundwood to do small repairs. He was often caught poaching salmon in some mountain stream but was always cheerful and unrepentant about it.

I formed some sort of liaison with Henry, the lead guitarist.

We fell passionately in love for a week but this experience was not connected with reality in any way. In the afternoons Caroline, Roderic, Camilla and I would go shopping. These musicians ate like horses and we spent a lot of time shopping. It was a most beautiful summer. We passed the days in a blaze of sunshine and shade, driving through country lanes, picking wild flowers to put on our kitchen table, which was the only place left for us to be, and drinking. We asked the Hamiltons, who used to own Roundwood, to dinner and Elizabeth cried when she saw the chaos that everything was in. Kieran and Frances, the landlords from El Paso, came and had a wonderful time.

Suddenly three weeks were up and it was time for the musicians to go home. Brian came back and was treated with great respect. He looked a bit worried when he saw the bales of hay in the hall, which had been used as a sound baffle device of some sort, but we had an extremely jolly last dinner. Everyone sped off in the morning, leaving me with some very mysterious tapes of our conversations since there had been microphones all over the house. It turned out that nothing had been private.

When we were alone, Caroline, Brian and I cleaned and scrubbed and washed and polished until soon Roundwood was back to normal. 'I think I'll get a local woman to help next time,' Brian said.

Brian and I went out together to have a drink and had a long talk about sex. He was very shy and took a long time to get to the point. 'You know I'm homosexual?' he said. I said that I had thought perhaps he was so and that many of my friends were and that I knew quite a lot about it. He looked enormously relieved.

'Have you told Desmond?' I asked him. 'He's awfully understanding.'

'No, no, no, I couldn't. I've never told anyone, except Roxanne.'

I suddenly realized how difficult it must be to be homosexual in a small Catholic country, where everybody knows everybody else and the church and your family would be awfully shocked. I wound my arms around his waist and gave him a big hug and a kiss. He looked pleased.

'That's nice,' he said.

'Why are you telling me all this now?' I asked him.

'I've fallen in love,' Brian replied, a note of pride in his voice. 'I've fallen in love with a boy from Dublin and he's coming down here next weekend.'

'Goody,' I said, 'that'll be lovely. What's his name?'

'Ginger,' Brian replied.

'What? He's got red hair?' I squeaked.

We got the giggles and went back to Roundwood very cheerful and jolly. I felt tremendously honoured that Brian had thought fit to confide in me, but slightly worried that he hadn't said anything to Desmond.

Ginger duly turned up and proved to be a perfectly nice young man with carroty-coloured hair. He was not stunningly handsome or madly witty, but he was friendly and pleasant. I put a battered teddy-bear on Brian's bed on the night he arrived, a relic of Brian's childhood, I thought.

We went for long walks up on the mountains, through tracts of bogland and low, clinging cloud, sometimes glimpsing County Offaly and, I thought, Birr Castle. We went to the mountain pub where Canis and Moira reigned and we sat round a blazing log fire in the evenings drinking

Mr Murphy's horrible wine. Brian was really happy, but controlled.

Several weekends passed in this way, and then three American girls, members of the Georgian Society in America, arrived to stay at Roundwood and help with the various projects that were under way. They were charming girls. The one that I got on best with was called Robin and was going to be an actress. Pugin also arrived, on his bicycle from Waterford. Pugin was really called Ian Lumley. He was eighteen years old, a member of the Irish Georgian Society and a student at Bolton Street, the architectural part of Dublin University. He was a very old-fashioned boy and he arrived on a very old-fashioned bicycle and he drank neither tea nor coffee nor alcohol. He opened his mouth and passed a remark about the architecture of Roundwood and Brian named him Pugin. It suited him.

There was a terrible job to be done in the park. The lovely land in front of the house was infested with ragwort and it all had to be pulled up by hand. Every bit of root had to be removed, or it just grew back again and somehow redoubled. Day after day we slaved away and it was a hellish job, but things done with Brian were always pleasurable, he made one laugh.

One day Robin said to me that she thought Brian seemed a bit sad, did I know why? I thought he had been rather quiet lately, but I hadn't noticed anything in particular. I asked him why and he said rather nonchalantly, 'Oh, Ginger thinks he doesn't want to see me any more and he is going to see a doctor about it.' This last obviously hurt because on top of everything Ginger must have thought that there was something wrong with his relationship with Brian. I said I was terribly sorry but that I was sure he would calm down and change his mind. He was far too fond of Brian to cut off the friendship so abruptly and cruelly. We looked at each other.

Chapter Twenty-Five

The Irish Georgian Society was putting on a production of *Sweeney Todd, the Demon Barber*. This was a great favourite with the members and was done every few years. This year Desmond was playing Dr Abdinabab and my friend Julian Lloyd was playing the young hero. I said to Brian that I would love to see it and could I please go up to Leixlip with him. He gave me a bit of a funny look and said yes, but that I'd have to look after myself and find myself somewhere to stay. Slightly puzzled, I said that was fine. I'd ring up Victoria and Julian, who lived at the Glebe in Leixlip at the foot of the castle drive, and ask them.

Next morning Brian and I said goodbye to the American girls – Pugin had already departed – and set off for Leixlip. About halfway there I asked Brian to stop the car in a hurry. I got out and was violently sick for several minutes. 'That's very odd,' I said to him, 'I hardly had anything to drink last night and I definitely haven't got a hangover. Why on earth was I sick and why do I feel so ill?'

When we got to Leixlip, we lost each other in the throngs of people, but I saw him at the performance, clearly enjoying himself enormously, joining in all the ritual barracking with the audience and laughing his head off. Afterwards there was a party and we smiled at each other affectionately over the room. 'Brian's in good form,' several people remarked to me.

'Yes, isn't he?' I replied.

The next morning Brian's car drew up at the Glebe.

'Are you coming?' he asked. 'I must be off now.'

'No,' I replied. 'It's Patrick Coynyngham's eighteenth birthday party at his mother's house. Don't you remember? You must come. He will be awfully disappointed if you don't.'

Brian looked a bit blank. 'No, I can't. I must go.'

'Well, darling,' I said, 'I'll see you tomorrow then. OK?' He drove away and I watched the car disappear.

Patrick's party was a proper 'do' and went on till late. For some reason his mother was very nice to me. I got rather drunk and danced a lot. We got back to the Glebe and rolled into bed in the small hours.

I had just got up the next day when the doorbell rang, a long peal. I tripped gaily down to open it and there stood Desmond's darling daughter, Marina. She was leaning on the doorpost, with one arm supporting herself, and her hair was hanging down covering her face. She looked such a picture of utter despair that I thought it was some kind of Guinness joke and said in quite a jolly voice, 'Whatever is the matter, Marina?'

She looked up slowly and her huge, blue eyes were full of tears. 'Brian's dead,' she said.

I reeled back and I could hear a keening noise, like a wail, coming from my throat and from hers.

Victoria and Julian came rushing down the stairs. 'What's the matter? Who's dead?' Victoria said.

We turned to her. 'Brian is dead,' I said.

Marina said, 'He killed himself in his car.'

Marina and I walked very slowly up the castle drive, as if we were old, to go and find Desmond and see what we could do. I felt completely detached from my body and sort of walked along beside it. We found Desmond in his office. He looked ghastly. Audrey, his secretary and Brian's old friend, was sitting at her typewriter with tears pouring down her cheeks. I went round and hugged her.

'Is it true?' I asked despairingly and looked at Desmond.

'Yes,' he said.

'What shall we do?' I asked.

Desmond said, 'Well, I've cabled John Tormey in America, who actually owns Roundwood, and told him. I've told him that you are going to look after the house and we'll see if that is all right with him.'

I swallowed.

'Now I think that you and Audrey must drive down to Roundwood and look after those nice American girls and sort out the police.'

Audrey and I got into her car and started a drive that seemed endless. It can't have taken more than two hours in fact, but time seemed to have become teased and tortured out into meaningless and endless moments. I suppose it was a nice day, but the green and luscious Irish countryside appeared to be like a boiling hot and arid desert somewhere in Mexico. We drove on and on and hardly spoke. The sun burned down and turned everything into a harsh red and yellow colour. At last we arrived at Roundwood. The girls were grouped around

Kelvin Webb, Penny's 'Pup', and the shaven-headed me at the Grove in the Seventies

Above, left: An unknown, Julian Atwood, Derek Fitzgerald, me and Penny
in the garden at the Grove
Above, right: Catherine Palmer, looking West Indian and very bonny

My dear and stylish friend Julian Ormsby Gore

Me – setting off from the Grove to the Den for the first time – with all my housekeeping equipment

A greyhound and me at the Den in the Seventies

Mark Palmer looking charismatic

Marianne Faithfull, Patrick and Marina Guinness and a friend in Ireland

John Michell – expounding

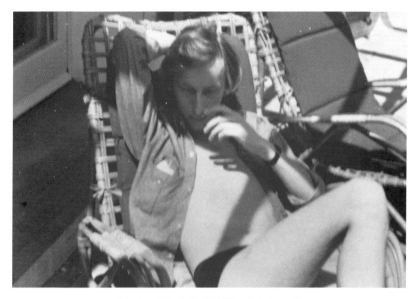

My dear friend, David Mlinaric, 'Monster'

The doyenne of the Grove, Penny Cuthbertson

Martha Mlinaric with her beautiful little daughter, Jessie

My friend Angus Wood (second right) and his aptly named band Out to Lunch

My children, Joshua and Caroline, having a laugh

My adored dog, Max, in 1991

the front door on the steps crying. The yard was full of policemen and their cars, and by the kitchen door was Brian's little car with his body still in it, sitting upright in the driving seat. As the garda saw us, a sort of low murmur went up, 'Henrietta Moraes'.

Audrey and I joined the weeping girls and put our arms around them and tried to comfort them. They all had little bits of a story to tell, of how they had had a perfectly ordinary dinner, of how they had said goodnight and gone to bed and of how one of them had heard Brian coming downstairs again at about two o'clock to take his dog, Dilly, out, but had thought nothing particular of it. One of them said, 'He left you a letter, Henrietta, but the garda found it and took it.'

I was utterly furious and went round to the yard. As I walked past Brian's car, I stumbled and fell into the side of it. 'I'm so sorry, darling,' I said. 'I didn't mean to do that.' I looked through the car window at Brian. He looked absolutely ordinary sitting there, not dead at all, rosy-cheeked and quite tranquil. I faced the policemen, who were looking at me in an odd way.

'You've taken my letter. Give it back to me at once. It's mine.' I trembled.

One of them said, 'I can't do that. I need it as evidence.'

I held out my hand. 'Give it to me.' Slowly he handed it over. They'd opened it and read it. My brain felt ice-white with rage, I could hardly breathe.

I unfolded it and read it as best I could. It had been written in a highly agitated state, with crossings-out and misspellings, and so was hard to read. It was a loving and apologetic letter, with a few requests and many affirmations of affection and love. But it was the letter of a man whose heart and spirit had

171

been broken and who had clearly had enough of life. I put it into my pocket with feelings of misery and heavy-heartedness such as I'd never had before.

I cannot remember very much of what followed until the funeral. People came and went, and Brian's family arrived. They were very angry and aggressive. Brian had left everything he possessed to the Irish Georgian Society, except for a bit of silver to a favourite niece; nothing to his mother or brothers. He left five hundred pounds to me and had given me a very pretty watch some time before, which turned out to have belonged to his father. The feeling of his family towards the rest of us was one of total hate, full of the deepest resentment. At the inquest one of his brothers came up to me, forced me up against a wall and said, 'Give me the watch back and we'll say no more about it.' I meekly handed it back, though it was precious to me. I didn't know what else to do. I had never seen a family fighting over an unsatisfactory will before.

The funeral was held on a sunny afternoon. Somehow I felt particularly bereft because the sun was shining and the world looked beautiful but I knew it wasn't. I put on a black dress and a little green and gold jacket and wondered how I was going to get through it. I stood and knelt and sat and prayed and sang and spoke as if from a different place and hoped the service would not go on too long or I would faint.

There were many people there, and afterwards we all went back to Roundwood. I was having some drinks when a now familiar, nightmare-like cry went up. 'Henrietta, the Molloys have taken your letter from Brian.' I had left the letter on my dressing table, just lying on the top, and it had not occurred to me that it might get stolen. Cold, white anger came over me and I found the same brother who had taken the watch, I knew it was him, and demanded and got my letter back. Eventually just a small nucleus of people remained sadly drinking red wine. The American girls, Desmond, Penny, Audrey and I, and a few others, were left in an atmosphere of melancholy and subdued misery.

Chapter Twenty-Six

I soon found myself alone and I hadn't really the first idea of
how to get through the time. There I was alone in a beautiful
house in the country with nobody to talk to or be with. Alone
in a house which had previously been a joy to me and where
there had been a person I loved. I couldn't decide what to do
when I got up in the morning or for the rest of the day and
night. I wandered about aimlessly in the house and the grounds.
Sometimes I took my dog for walks, or went a mile up the
road to the little shop and bought my daily needs. I did not
have a car and Mountrath was not accessible to me. There
didn't seem to be any neighbours. Brian's local friends – the
schoolmistress in Mountrath, for instance – shunned me,
nobody came to call. I had an old-fashioned idea that lots of
local people would come and somehow comfort me in my
bereavement, but they didn't.

One evening I saw two figures approaching the house. One
was the man who rented the park for his cattle, Oliver Phelan.
By his side walked a short figure, with her hair done up in a

bun and with her eyes heavily underlined and wearing high-heeled sandals. She was reminiscent of the Sixties. After we had greeted each other, they said how sorry they were to hear about Brian. Then they said they were going to town to do a bit of shopping and have a drink. Would I like to come? Would I? I assented eagerly, and that was the beginning of a long friendship. Almost every evening for some years the Phelans would roll up at about six and we would take off for Mountrath, shop and have some drinks at El Paso. For me it was a real lifeline.

They had several children. One was called Con. He had been deprived of oxygen at birth and suffered brain damage. For years he had been unable to walk or talk, but his parents had saved up enough money to go to America and get treatment from a Dr Dent. Dent believed in the constant manipulation of such children, that they should be encouraged to crawl and move their limbs as much as possible, and Con had improved enormously and could now walk and talk quite a lot. He could say my name, Henrietta.

One afternoon that autumn I was sitting outside the front door on the steps drinking some wine and another lifeline appeared. A car appeared up the drive and out of it stepped a charming and beautiful woman, who said, 'Hello, I'm Kitty Hamilton. I hope you don't mind me calling.'

I rose to my feet and offered her a glass of wine, even though it was half past three in the afternoon, and she accepted. We sat and talked for an hour or so and I really liked her and found her totally sympathetic. Her husband, Paul, was a first cousin of Chetwood Hamilton, whose family had owned Roundwood, and she had many happy memories of the place. She lived in a house called Moyne some miles away, and she asked me to lunch on Sunday and said that she would collect me and bring me home. What kindness. I watched her drive away and felt sad.

I had not realized the complexity and durability of bereavement and grief. I had known other people who had killed themselves, but they had been more distant from me. The effect of Brian's death was profound and catastrophic. It haunted me with feelings of guilt and depression. I drank as much as I possibly could.

People came to visit me, at weekends mostly, and I would sit for hours with them, thrashing out the details of what had happened just before Brian's death and thinking how, had I been at Roundwood, I could perhaps have prevented it. Extraordinary details of his behaviour emerged. How someone had seen him carrying a bit of hosepipe around one afternoon. How someone else had seen him fiddling about underneath his car. I realized that the drive up to Leixlip had been a sort of dress rehearsal for his suicide and that was why I had been so sick and why he hadn't been too keen on my going up with him. He must have drilled the holes in the floor and fixed up the hosepipe before we even left Roundwood. Brian had got hold of some sleeping pills from a chemist that week. It was all so well planned and deliberate and so well hidden, that he was bound to have succeeded. He had never made a fuss or shouted and screamed like most of us do. He had never raised a suspicion in anybody's mind as to what his intentions were and so he took us all by surprise. Gradually the painful of sense of guilt wore off but the feeling of loss persisted.

Pugin visited Roundwood a lot at this time. He came on his bicycle all the way from Dublin and was a tower of strength and a constant support. I know that in the end I bored him rigid with my endless replaying of the horrible scenes, but he was as efficacious for me as a friendly therapist.

I never really stopped being lonely at Roundwood. When I took the dogs out in the afternoon, I would return to the house hoping and praying for a visitor to be there, but I mostly came round the corner to an empty drive. I started thinking of my time there as a sort of solitary confinement and perhaps good for the soul. What it was good for was my drinking. I had made friends with Moira and Canice up at the Village Inn in Coleraine. I would telephone Moira and ask her to bring me some Special Brew and some whisky and she would drive down from the mountains with them. They kept me going. Sometimes old men in long black coats and cloth caps would appear, like wraiths walking through the park. They would produce a bottle of poteen from an overcoat pocket with a solemn warning not to drink it all at once, it would drive me mad. I didn't take much notice of the warnings, and consequently thought I heard a banshee crying.

The days I remember with the most pain were the days of constant rainfall. There is a particular sort of murky yellow rain that falls in County Laoise. It is heavy and continuous and falls all day long from a leaden yellow sky.

Of course there were jolly times too, when the house was full of visitors. One Christmas my friends Denny and Theodora Cordell and their children and friends rented the house and I stayed and made myself useful.

I had a telephone call one day from Paddy Maloney of the Chieftains. He was an old friend of Desmond and Penny, whom I had often met in the past. He said he fancied a weekend at Roundwood and that he would like to play for the people here and there. What did I think? I thought it would be marvellous. I arranged with Moira and Canis that Paddy would come and play in their pub one night, and the next night we would have a party at Roundwood.

The word went round and people became rather excited. The Village Inn was packed when we arrived. Paddy had brought his wife and children and we were all very pleased with the outing. He played and he played and we went home tired and happy. The next morning I met him on the drive. We were both staggering along, breathing in deep gulps of fresh air and looking pale and wan. 'I think we'd better go to the pub, Paddy,' I said, 'and down a few Guinnesses.'

That evening County Laoise arrived at Roundwood and Paddy played his pipes all over the house – from the gallery, on the stairs, in the kitchen. It was magic.

Desmond and Penny often visited. Penny and I started a flower bed, planting clematis, honeysuckle and a rosebush. Desmond's son Patrick and his wife Liz visited me, but what I remember most is being alone and missing Brian.

I spent five years altogether at Roundwood. I felt a fierce loyalty to Desmond and Penny, which gave me the courage to stick it out. When Desmond said that the house had to be sold, I felt a sense of relief.

Chapter Twenty-Seven

I went to Hong Kong one more time as Suki was pregnant again and said she needed me. When I got there, I found that she had made friends with some seriously ghastly neighbours in Shek-O, who made no bones of the fact that they despised me because I was poor. She had also started drinking brandy in the afternoon and didn't seem to need me at all. So I went back to Ireland, where I found my dear old bitch Den was dying.

I was staying with Victoria and Julian Lloyd at the Glebe in Leixlip and, after the visit from the vet, we gave Den an honourable funeral and a romantic resting place in Penny's kitchen garden, under a wild rose bush.

Denny Cordell had bought a house in Ireland called Corries. As he and Theadora were going to be away all summer, he asked me to go and look after it. It was a nice house and he had lots of horses and a very smart stable with a covered riding school, and I went there with pleasure. There was a cook, Moira, and a housekeeper, Ina, as well as a rather unpleasant girl who was supposed to look after the garden. In the yard there were two heavenly Irishmen who took care of the horses, Jim and his brother Martin.

There was a cob mare in the field by the house who had a foal that had to be weaned. Jim put me in charge of Mrs Cob, whom Denny had bought from some travellers. When I first met her, she had hairy ankles and a rough, shaggy mane, but underneath you could see that she had more than a touch of class. I fell devotedly in love with her and we became the best of friends.

My first task was to milk her when her foal was taken away and I viewed this with some trepidation. But I'd milked a goat, hadn't I? I told Jim I was nervous. He laughed. So I set off with a halter in one hand and a bowl in the other. I gave Mrs Cob a carrot and tied her up and milked her. It was easy, and she didn't seem to mind one bit. I had a bowl full of creamy mare's milk when I'd finished, which triggered off some memory of Ghengis Khan's wild Mongolian hordes drinking mare's milk in the Gobi Desert on their way to invade Russia. So I sat on the fence talking to Mrs Cob, and as the sun began to set I drank down her delicious milk.

I set about getting Mrs Cob and myself in order. Apparently she had never really been ridden before, and definitely not bridled and saddled up. I started by hogging her mane and trimming her ankles neatly and then I brushed her coat until she shone like a conker. Jim looked on admiringly. Then I saddled her with Theodora's saddle and found a bridle that fitted. I mounted and off we went. She had never been out on the road without blinkers before, so that every little thing – the odd leaf or road sign glimpsed out of the corner of her eye, an old sack or a dog – would startle her. But she possessed great equanimity and we progressed along the roads and lanes quite trimly. Until we got to a certain house which she would not pass. Nothing I could do would move her on and I had to dismount and lead her past it, clucking gently all the while.

We soon got used to each other and went for long rides every day and we began to get into condition. We both lost a lot of weight and our tummies disappeared and our hair shone with health. Jim suggested that we put her between the shafts of the little trap and this was an enormous success. We bowled along the lanes, mostly at a canter, because that was the pace she liked best. What a pleasure it was that summer to fly along the dappled, leafy lanes of County Carlow, nonchalantly smoking a home-grown joint and watching the intelligently twitching ears of my fine mare.

The next thing we had to find out was whether Mrs Cob could jump and if not to teach her to. One afternoon in the yard we rigged up a small jump. Martin climbed up and set her at it. She didn't have a clue, walked up and knocked it over. We made it a bit higher and this time the penny dropped and she leaped over a bit clumsily. The next time was better and she suddenly got the hang of it and started flying over. We made it higher and higher, and over she went. She was such a natural star, Mrs Cob, that you couldn't help but love and respect her.

One morning in early autumn I went riding out on Mrs Cob with Jim, Martin and the racehorses. It was slightly misty and damp. As we clattered along, Mrs Cob had to canter quite fast to keep up with the much bigger racehorses. We turned into a stubble field, rode up the hill and turned to gallop right round it. Mrs Cob and I were left far, far behind as the others swept effortlessly on. We were galloping downhill when it happened. She slipped on the wet stubble and I lost my balance. For what seemed an eternity I hung sideways, off balance, and then crashed. I hit the ground at about twenty-eight miles an hour, my shoulder taking the full force. I lay there unable to move and I knew something serious had happened. I was alone in the field, everyone else had disappeared, and I had to force myself to get up. I tried but the left-hand side of my body on which I had fallen kept on dragging me back to earth again. I was completely lopsided and had no control over myself at all.

I made a tremendous effort. I felt no pain and was determined not to be found by the lads lying helpless on the ground. I got to my knees and very carefully stood up. I didn't feel like me at all. I felt like an alien, a very delicate and clumsy invader. At this moment, as I stood there, a tiny little woman carrying a bottle of brandy and a tumbler came through the hedge. She said, 'I saw what happened, I was watching, it was terrible. I've brought you some of this.' She indicated the brandy and I managed to thank her and say I'd be very grateful for a drink. She poured out a full glass, which I drained down, and immediately I felt more human.

Jim and Martin swept round the corner. They were laughing until they saw my face and my helpless arm and shoulder dangling from my body. 'I think I've broken my arm,' I said in as normal a voice as I could, 'and I think I should get to hospital now.' Jim looked disbelieving, aghast and resigned, and turned to Martin to give him instructions.

I do not remember much of the drive to hospital or my arrival. I remember some X-rays being taken, which was agonizing because I couldn't do any of the things that they wanted me to do with my arm. Then I was surrounded by doctors and nurses talking earnestly to me. They told me that my arm and shoulder were in a terrible mess and there was nothing they could do. So they were sending me to the Kilkenny Orthopaedic Hospital, where all the injured jump jockeys went and where I would find the best man in Ireland to fix me up.

At Kilkenny I was looked after by a doctor called Merlyn White, which seemed like a good omen, and he was adorable. He was immensely excited by my case. 'I haven't seen anything like this for years,' he said as he looked at the X-rays. 'What a mess. Wonderful.' He told me that I'd broken my collar-bone twice, dislocated and shattered my shoulder and broken the upper arm to sort of balance it. I told him that I knew he was the only man in Ireland who could help me and that I completely trusted him.

The road to recovery was slow. I was completely immobilized for ten days and only after a very earnest and heartfelt bout of begging was I allowed to creep out of bed to go to the lavatory by myself. However, I have always rather enjoyed being in hospital and being completely looked after, and I have always loved Irish nurses and got on with them particularly well. The sister on my ward was the epitome of an old-fashioned, no-nonsense or self-pity, but deeply understanding and kind warrior-nurse. I adored her. She let me smoke and drink Special Brew and go round the ward talking to all the other patients to my heart's content.

Slowly my arm and shoulder began to heal and I was able to wheel the tea trolley around. I had a fair amount of pain, but I was always given pain-killing drugs when I asked for them. Martin and Jim came to see me a lot and brought me in cigarettes and drink. Denny and Theodora and their children visited, and Kitty Hamilton, who came all the way from County Laoise, once took me away for a weekend, which was heavenly.

After three months, my guru, Mr Merlyn White, judged it was time to take off the plaster and remove from my shoulder an enormous pin which had held everything together. Then the physiotherapist went to work on me and this was the most painful time of all. I had to stand facing a wall and to creep my fingers up from knee level to shoulder height. I couldn't get above middle-thigh level, not for ages, and I nearly despaired. Raising my arm above my head seemed inconceivable but I was forced to go on trying and made very slow progress. I used my legs a lot though and skipped about the place. The result of this was that I pulled my Achilles tendon and had to have a plaster on my left leg.

A few weeks before Christmas I was discharged and Victoria collected me and took me back to the Glebe. I was pretty miserable. I had nowhere to live, my leg was in plaster and I had no money. Victoria and Julian put me up and put up with me. They were extremely kind but I knew my presence was a strain and I couldn't think what to do next. Monster saved my bacon, not for the first time, and sent me money to get to England. I had one last Christmas in Ireland. Christmas Day at the castle and Boxing Day at the Glebe. I was sad because I had no money to buy Christmas presents.

Chapter Twenty-Eight

I returned to England with Desmond and Penny. Desmond said he would sock me a week at the Chelsea Arts Club and then it was up to me to arrange my life and find somewhere to live. It was such an extreme situation for me to start from scratch and settle everything in a week that somehow I wasn't frightened. Monster, who had telephoned his sister to find out what I should do, told me that I had to go to the DSS and the housing people and get a medical certificate to say I couldn't work. Penny gave me a list of telephone numbers to ring for possible lodgings. Strangely, one was at number 11 Apollo Place, just opposite where I had once lived and I determined to try this one first. A woman's voice answered.

I said, 'I have just come to England from Ireland and I'm looking for somewhere to live. I have been given your number and I wonder if you have got anywhere?'

There was a short pause. 'Well,' said the voice. 'Oddly enough I have got a room, in Edith Grove.'

I said, 'Oh, I'd love to see it. Edith Grove, that's nice and handy for everything.'

We met outside a house in Edith Grove and went up to the first floor, where we entered a medium-sized room. It was at the back of the house and looked out over the gardens. It faced west and the late January sun was pouring through the sash window. I could hear a blackbird singing. The room was clean and the walls were cream-coloured, magnolia actually. I stood quietly for a few seconds and then said, 'I think I could be very happy here. May I have it?' I went back to the office, which overlooked my old house at 9 Apollo Place, and had a sort of interview. I gave Desmond, Penny, Martha and Monster as references and tried hard to make a good impression. I explained that I had to go to the DSS and fix everything up with the housing people, and that in the meantime I was staying at the Chelsea Arts Club for a week and would they please let me know?

The rest of that week was a slow nightmare. It was terribly cold. My leg was still in plaster and I had to wait for hours on end in government offices in long queues and explain my predicament to many different people over and over again. Mostly, people were very nice to me, nice but resigned. But once somebody was unduly sharp and to my surprise I burst into tears. Not being that sort of person, I had not realized the efficacy of tears before. They worked a treat and that particular bit of business was settled very fast. Eventually I had all the bits of paper I needed to get my rent paid and to get an unemployment giro every week. I had a couple of days of my week left and waited breathlessly for news about my room.

I spoke to Penny on the telephone.

'They really like you very much, Hen,' she said. 'But there

is one thing. They think that you drink too much and they'll only let you have the room if you do something like go to AA.'

'Oh.' I was rather surprised. 'Oh well, in that case I'll go. I'll go round and tell them so.'

I went round to the office and said that I was willing to go to AA, and they said I could have the room. I was absolutely delighted and went off to an AA meeting in order to keep my end of the bargain. I knew nothing about this organization and in any case I didn't believe that I drank too much, so I attended these meetings for about three months without taking anything in. I stopped drinking though.

One rather jolly thing happened during my week at the Arts Club, and that was an Irish Georgian Society charity ball. It was on the theme of Morocco, and Monster was doing the décor. I helped with this, just did what I was told. It was held at Christie's and the rooms looked absolutely fabulous when they were finished. I was to appear as a beggar with a begging bowl and collect money for the Irish Georgians. My partner was Little Nell, who later went to New York and started an enormously successful club. We sat on either side of the stairs and I shouted 'Baksheesh' so vociferously that I embarrassed Penny. After the ball I found myself alone and had to walk all the way back to Chelsea. I got the most enormous and painful blister on my heel under the plaster of Paris. Next morning I went to St Stephen's Hospital and they cut the plaster off, tut-tutting like anything.

My room was unfurnished. Penny said, 'Come on, we'll go to the Reject Shop and get some coconut matting. Let's measure the room up.' Later Penny saw a double bed and mattress lying in the road in Redcliffe Gardens, which we excitedly inspected and then lugged to Edith Grove. A load of furniture came from Martha and Monster's store in the country, including knives and forks, a lemon squeezer, a chest of drawers, four van Gogh-like chairs, blankets, sheets and towels, and a very nice blue-and-white-print tablecloth of a Chinese scene. Slowly the makings of a little home were assembled. I moved in before the electricity could be connected and spent the first few days contemplating my treasures by candlelight. Monster gave me a radio and I became an avid listener to Radio 4.

A quiet time of adjustment followed. It was strange being back in London, in Chelsea which I had known so well. It was weird living in one room after the grandeur of Roundwood and it was difficult to live on income support.

The house was full of old ladies. Chelsea Housing Association is a sort of charity and looks after needy people. On the top floor there was a lady called Trudie, who seemed quite fierce. She knitted a lot and listened to classical music. On her front door was a pottery notice saying 'Cave Canem', 'Beware of the Dog'. She turned out to have an ironic vein and to be rather kind. Opposite me there was an Irish lady, who used to be a nurse. She was waiting to go back to Ireland and live with her brother. Downstairs were Margaret, a monthly nurse, and an old stalwart from another era called Nanny Baines. Nobody knew how old she was but her memory was beginning to go and she would often leave the house without her key and hang about outside the front door waiting for someone to come home and let her in. When communication did take place, she turned out to be kindly but repressive. She didn't have the slightest idea of creature comforts and lived in a cold room with bare overhead lighting, a one-bar electric fire and no television. I've noticed that when nannies retire, they often don't have the slightest idea of how to look after themselves.

Eve, the doyenne of 18 Edith Grove, lived in the basement. She was nudging her nineties and had lived there since the war and remembered the bombs being dropped. She knew everyone in the street and what was worth knowing about them. She was immensely frank in her speech and demeanour and loved animals and gardens. She was fond of her gin and of a joke and regaled me with many tales of the Grove.

Once I had got used to my room, I fell into a kind of a routine. I explored the neighbourhood in detail and spent many hours in my local Oxfam shop, finding really good bargains in snakeskin shoes and cashmere sweaters. I went for short urban walks and watched a lot of television, especially in the afternoons. I found it quite addictive. I was drinking again, nothing like as much as I did in Ireland but still at every given opportunity.

I went to stay with my friends Guy and Beatrix Nevill, who had got married when I was still in Ireland. We were doing a bit of gardening one afternoon and Guy suddenly said, 'You're an awfully good gardener, Madre. Would you like to do my sister's garden?' And that is how I became a gardener and discovered a new passion.

I went round to Durham Place where Guy's sister, Angela, lived with her friend Billy Keating. Angela was perfectly civil to me and quite keen to take me on, but Billy was more difficult.

'How do I know that you are any more reliable than Guy is?' he demanded. 'After all, you are his friend.'

I was very taken aback. 'Well, you'll just have to take me on trust,' I replied, 'and wait and see if I turn up or not.' I was cross.

Angela was soothing. 'Come and give it a try-out,' she said, and I agreed to.

Durham Place is at the end of Smith Street off the King's Road. The houses are large and Georgian and very pretty. Angela and Billy ran an art business from their house and received clients in it every day. They also entertained a lot and had a lunch party most days of the week. I saw that the garden would have to be a credit to the house to impress the clients who might happen to look out of the window.

I spent the first few months tidying up and weeding and restoring some kind of order and harmony into the garden. It had masses of day lilies and not much else except an outstanding feature in two magnificent camellia trees trained up against a wall. One day Angela and Billy said, 'The garden looks awfully pretty, Henrietta. Would you like to have a free hand and do it over completely?' I was thrilled. Billy said, 'I'd like to have some stone steps at the end of the garden leading up to a pergola. Perhaps also we could widen and curve the right-hand bed and put a small circular bed in the middle. What do you think?'

I said, 'Lovely, how exciting.'

Billy asked, 'Do you know anyone who could do the work?'

I thought of Charlie and Mickey and arranged a meeting. Billy and I had become firm friends by now and, having found out that my favourite tipple was Special Brew, he arranged that there should be an endless supply for me in the kitchen.

Charlie came and scored a big hit with Billy and the work started. I ordered many bags of top-grade garden earth, bone-meal, blood and fishmeal and waited impatiently while the beds were widened and the steps were laid. The front of the pergola was made out of lattice-work, and I thought, Aha, roses, old-fashioned roses, and clematis. I thought the wall at the back of the house, which caught all the sun, and those on one side of the garden, yearned to be smothered with roses, honeysuckle and more clematis.

At last the building work was finished. Some impressive stone steps led to a charming little pergola, where people could lunch and have drinks, and a long curved bed with a little circular bed in its middle stood waiting to be adorned with plants and flowers. But first everything had to be dug, dug deep and dug well. Dug so that nothing remained but new garden soil spiced with blood and bone. And worms, I wished for many worms. I dug and forked and shook and sifted and mixed and mucked until I had a satisfactory, dark brown, chocolaty, light and friable, but rich and sustaining, amalgam of soil ready to be planted.

I had had no actual experience of such an undertaking before, but I was determined to do my very best and strangely enough had a strong belief in my capabilities. I had been to the Chelsea Flower Show that year and had collected the best classic catalogues that I could find from the stalls. Catalogues such as the David Austin handbook of roses and the David Austin handbook of hardy plants were mines of information, beautifully written and full of the information I needed.

I holed up in Edith Grove for a weekend and made out lists of what I wanted. Just on paper the roses were intoxicating.

'Gloire de Dijon', an old favourite of the cottage gardens of
yesterday, where it was known as 'Old Glory Rose'.

'Etoile de Hollande, Climbing', the climbing sport of a
famous old hybrid tea.

'Château de Clos-Vougeot, Climbing', flowers of the darkest
rich velvet-crimson which do not fade.

'Madame Butterfly, Climbing', a sport of Ophelia.

'Mermaid', large, single, sulphur-yellow flowers with wide,
elegant petals and amber-coloured stamens.

'Zéphirine Drouhin', fragrant, deep rose-pink flowers.

'Albertine', reddish-salmon buds opening into large,
coppery-pink, almost double flowers with a strong scent.

'Rambling Rector', a strong, dense, twiggy growth smothered with small, creamy-white, semi-double flowers. Delicious fragrance.

As I made out my list, my mouth watered with anticipation of
the beauty of things to come.

For my hardy plants, I wanted an old-fashioned look again,
and responded eagerly to suggestions of hollyhocks, alchemilla,
aquilegia, campanula, aster, delphinium, digitalis, geranium,
gypsophila, hosta, lavender, melissa, nepeta, peonies, poppies,
phlox, potentilla, primula, golden rod, violets, periwinkles and
violas. I had been reading Gertrude Jekyll and Vita Sackville-
West, and my imagination was illumined by visions of a vast,
ranging flower bed billowing and frothing in all shades of blue
and purple and golden yellow.

Billy and Angela approved my lists and I sent off my orders
to the nursery and waited impatiently for the plants to arrive.
Billy and Angela turned out to be almost perfect employers in
the sense that they very seldom interfered with my work, but

simply let me get on with it. It was a real joy to visualize ideas and then be able to put them into practice.

The herbaceous plants arrived first in September and I was enthralled by the process of choosing their sites, carefully positioning them and then digging in and planting them. I tried hard to get all the angles right and ensure a satisfactory view of each plant. Gradually the bed began to fill up and look like something. The central bed was to be a little circular herb garden and was divided into three sections in radials from the centre. I filled it with thyme and balm, chives and parsley, two types of mint and, in the centre, wallflowers.

The roses arrived just before Christmas, and gave me my greatest shiver of excitement. They were, as is proper, bare-rooted and packed in big plastic bags. As I gazed at their dead-looking black twigs, I thought it would be a real miracle if they ever grew. Some of the roses went by the walls and some went into Versailles tubs on the steps of the pergola, and around the back door from the house to the garden.

I had planted lots of bulbs at the beginning of September, daffodils and narcissi, early and late tulips and snowdrops, and now I waited anxiously for at least one of them to appear. When I saw the first tender green tip poke through the earth, I almost wept with relief. January was a dead month for the garden and I stayed at home, but when I went back to Durham Place in February all sorts of things were happening. It was a very sheltered garden, protected from cold winds. Little clumps of miniature daffodils and crocuses nodded at me cheerily, and the tulips were poking above the ground. During February I watched the roses like a hawk, and at the beginning of March I saw, to my great pleasure and joy, that a leaf or two had begun to bud.

The garden progressed much in the way that I had planned. Snowdrops gave way to daffodils and then primroses, violets, tulips, wallflowers, and by summer everything was in full bloom. The 'Gloire de Dijon' opened up into great globules of pale pinkish yellow touched with gold at the centre. The 'Albertine' and the 'Mermaid' twined lovingly into the trellis of the pergola and a large, double-flowered white clematis and a honeysuckle climbed up alongside them. Lupins, foxgloves and hollyhocks nodded imperially at each other, and yellow Welsh poppies and celestially blue Himalayan poppies provided pools of colour. There were also groups of white marguerites and several bush roses bought on the spur of the moment at Covent Garden. Along the edge of the curved bed, set in among the old brick edging, yellow and purple violas jostled each other, while in the Versailles pots on the pergola steps clumps of 'Bowles' Black' violets looked mysteriously back at me, nestling down among the roots of the roses.

It was a hot summer and I had to do an awful lot of watering, defying the hose-pipe ban to water for at least an hour each day. The herbs all grew very well and were healthy. The 'Château de Clos-Vougeot' did not flower until the end of July and when its huge, dark red flowers unfolded, the scent was overwhelming. I had placed it close to the 'Rambling Rector', which suddenly burst into hundreds of small and very sweetly scented flowers at about the same time.

I did have some failures. One or two plants simply did not take to the conditions or like their neighbours, but in the main it was a lovely show.

I had made friends with some birds, a pair of robins and a pair of blackbirds. They used to appear every time I came into the garden, until at last they became quite tame and friendly and would watch me working. The robins performed the classic gesture that you see on so many Christmas cards of perching on the handle of my spade and regarding me cheekily. The blackbirds brought their babies to see me and I was very touched. As for their natures, the tiny and frail-looking robin could beat the sleek, robust and much bigger bird into a cocked hat when it came to a question of aggression.

I received many compliments on my gardening from all sorts of people, and I was pleased and proud. One summer Billy gave a party to show the garden off, but it poured with rain and as a spectacle it was ruined. For three years I gardened almost every day, and I had many pleasant days there. I went in for a lot of contemplation. Special Brew in hand, I would stare at my work and see where it could be improved and where it was satisfactory. I puzzled Angela, who thought I was not working and would call down from her office window, 'Enjoying a Special Brew, what?' Billy and I had long chats sitting in the garden, usually over a stiff gin and tonic, and I enjoyed these very much.

Chapter Twenty-Nine

Beatrix's daughter Rose owned a miniature long-haired dachshund bitch called Vixen. Vixen was adorable. She was very fierce and barked loudly at all strangers, and if she could get near enough she would bite them neatly on the ankle. She was black and tan, with a tan muzzle and two tan eyebrows seemingly raised in quizzical regard. She had a big bushy tail and silky blonde breeches. Her front paws were huge and pudgy and cried out to be kissed.

I loved her from the minute I saw her, and she took to me in quite an unrestrained way. She had a fiercely independent nature and was proud and knew her own worth. This seems to be a characteristic of dachshunds.

One day when I went round to see Beatrix, the Brazilian cleaning lady told me that Vixen was under Rose's bed and seemed unable to walk. I rushed upstairs and found her shivering under the bed, utterly miserable and able only to scrabble about. I picked her up very carefully and took her downstairs and gave her a drink of water, which she lapped up desperately.

When Beatrix came in, I said, 'Poor little Vixen.'

Beatrix said quickly, 'Why, what's the matter?' She looked at Vixen. 'Oh dear, poor little dog.'

We tore round to the vet, who was an Irish Zen Buddhist, and were lucky because nobody was in the waiting-room. He examined her very carefully and said, 'She's ruptured one of the discs in her vertebrae, some of the liquid has leaked out. She must have complete rest for some time. I'll let you have a cage from the surgery. It's about three foot by six and you must keep her in it till she can walk properly again.' So we went home and Vixen was incarcerated.

A few weeks later Beatrix said to me, 'Madre, would you have Vixen at Edith Grove for a bit? I need a bit of time off.' So Vixen came to live with me. I put her in her cage with blankets and cushions and soon learned why Beatrix had requested some time off. Vixen watched me constantly, every move I made she supervised, and if I read a book or watched television I could feel her glowing, reproachful eyes boring into me. It was ghastly. I've never felt so guilty in all my life.

One night I could bear it no more and lifted her out of her prison and into my bed. Strangely enough, from that time on she began to recover and could soon walk and run about quite freely. I had bought a bicycle and, after overcoming a natural fear of the traffic, I took to putting Vixen in the front basket and transporting her everywhere. I took her to work at Durham Place, where she had an enormous success with everyone but Angela. I once saw Billy curtsying to her. Eventually Rose wanted her back and so I sadly let her go, but when Vixen's disc ruptured again, once more I was asked to take her. I said that I could only have her if I could keep her, as I found the process of giving her back too painful. Rose, like a very good girl, agreed and Vixen came back to Edith Grove.

Vixen and I had an idyllically happy relationship. We went everywhere together, out for walks, away for the weekend, off to work, until the most terrible thing happened. One morning, as I was getting up and Vixen was sitting in her usual chair by the open window and looking out into the garden, an insolent pigeon appeared and started to strut up and down as if to challenge her. I took no particular notice as this sort of thing often happened, but when I left the room to go to the bathroom, Vixen jumped out of the window in a sporting attempt to catch the pigeon. She fell two floors into a concrete area and broke her back. I went back to the vet, who could not X-ray her for a couple of days but looked extremely grave when I told him what had happened.

She was kept in the vet's surgery for three days and I went to visit her each day. A nice girl brought her out to me. She was wrapped up tightly in a blanket. I sat by her side and talked gently to her and brushed her ears with a little brush and told her how much I loved her. I felt sick with misery. When the X-ray results came through, Beatrix and I went to the vet together. He said her back was broken badly, the prognosis was bad, she would never walk again and would always be in pain. Beatrix and I looked at each other. That was it, then. Forlornly we went into the surgery and the vet prepared the lethal injection. We all said goodbye to her and I told her how much everybody loved her and that she was the best little dog in the world. Beatrix cried, the vet cried, but I couldn't. Just as Mr Sullivan was about to inject Vixen with the hypodermic needle, she made one last typical and heroic gesture. She tried to bite him.

Chapter Thirty

In the months that followed I was heartbroken. I kept looking round for Vixen or thinking that she was at my heels. I couldn't get used to her absence. I felt numb and cold, lonely and dispirited. The zest had gone from my life. Eventually I was persuaded to get another puppy and I settled on a red, long-haired dachshund bitch from the north. She was the only bitch I could find, and I hadn't seen her when I collected her from the breeder. She was very, very small and very sweet. She came into the room, gambolling and tumbling after Mrs O'Neill, vainly trying to bite her slippers. She came over to where I sat on the floor, and nosed and licked my face. My heart warmed to her. Mrs O'Neill said, 'You don't have to take her, you know.' But it was too late for me by then. I already loved this tiny creature. I called her Phoenix, because there was an X in the name.

We settled in together but in truth Phoenix was never entirely well, she was more like a semi-invalid. She never grew very much and was so small that she tired very, very quickly. When I took her for walks, I had to carry her most of the way. She slept a lot more than is usual and never really invented her own games with the ball and other little toys that I bought her. She had a good appetite, though. I took her everywhere in my bicycle basket, as I had taken Vixen, and she was supremely happy looking out at the world from her high vantage point. I loved her but I always had to be very careful with her.

At about this time I began to feel ill. I often had nausea and sometimes got a sharp pain in my chest. It was rather like having a permanent hangover. My spirits were low but in an insidious sort of way. I began to feel very negative about everything, but this negativity was not so much conscious as a feeling that underlay everything. A drink or two would cheer me up.

I went out for a Chinese dinner with Martha and Monster, and moaned to them. I kept on saying that I didn't see the point of life and that I felt awful and I didn't know what was going to happen. The next day Monster said to me that he didn't think that I was very well and would I come with him to see his doctor, Annie Coxon. I was slightly surprised, but thought it was very kind of Monster to worry about me and I agreed.

We sat in the waiting-room in Harley Street and a pretty woman with reddish-blonde hair came into the room. Monster got to his feet and they kissed. He introduced us to each other and we went upstairs. Annie examined me, thumping away at my liver. I thought she said that it seemed to be all right and I felt rather pleased. She made an appointment for me the following week and took some blood samples. I rushed downstairs to Monster, shouting, 'Annie says that there is nothing wrong with my liver.' I half heard Annie say, 'I didn't actually say that, you know.' The next week I went back with Jane Rainey and I asked Annie if it would be all right to go to Ireland with Marina. She said yes, but that I should take it easy. She also said that she had to go away herself, to some place like Saudi Arabia to visit a patient, and that I would see her when I got back.

Marina and Phoenix and I caught the ferry to Dun Laoghaire and went to the house she had rented quite near Leixlip. After a few days I was invited to Kerry, where Oliver Musker and lots of Ormsby Gores were staying by the seaside with all their children. I went with Phoenix and we had a lovely time on the sands. Jane was there with some of her children and we shared a tent in the garden.

When I got back to Marina, I thought she seemed somehow rather upset. She cried when I had a drink of Pernod that I had bought on the boat. The telephone rang and Marina answered it. It was Monster.

'He wants to talk to you,' Marina said, holding out the receiver.

I said, 'Hi, Monster,' in a jolly voice.

'I've got something to tell you.'

'Yes, what is it?'

Monster replied in a very neutral voice, 'You've got cirrhosis of the liver. Annie asked me to tell you because she had to go away.'

I sat on the floor and said, 'Could you say that again?' He repeated it and I suddenly felt numb and cold and very serious.

'But doesn't that kill you?' I asked.

'Well, yes, it does if you drink.'

When it came down to this basic point, I discovered, rather

to my astonishment, that I did want to live and so I resolved then and there to give up alcohol. I thought that I could just do it. I came back to London, very shaken up and uncertain of everything. I saw Annie once a week and tried to listen to what she had to say. She turned out to be a most potent psychologist with an instinctive understanding of my rebellious nature. She never actually told me that I was forbidden to drink. She said, 'Maybe next summer you can have a glass of champagne on a special occasion.' Subtle things that I didn't react to. I struggled along like this for some months. I felt very ill and unhappy. One day I went to see Bill Davidson, my NHS doctor, a very dear man whom I had known for many years. We talked and he suddenly said, 'You can't do this alone, Henrietta.'

'What do you mean?'

'Just that. You can't do this alone.'

I thought a lot about what Bill had said and in the end went back to the same self-help group that I had been to before. In many ways my life was hell. I felt too ill to work and I had all this time on my hands that I was used to spending in drinking. Drinking with people in pubs, in clubs, in restaurants and alone at home. I had very little money because I was not working. It was winter and cold. I'm not sure what impelled me to go to all the group meetings that I went to. I suppose boredom was one reason, and there was some mysterious impulse which simply turned my footsteps in that direction. I would plod along unwillingly and grudgingly, but nevertheless I would turn up night after night. I didn't enjoy it, in fact I hated it. I loathed the way that everybody looked happy, while I was the exception. They kissed each other when they met, looked pleased to see each other, talked and even laughed.

I couldn't understand it. What was there to laugh about? As far as I was concerned, life was black and tragic and I had lost my best friend, booze.

I sat through meeting after meeting, half listening, half chafing at the bit, longing for the allotted time to be up and glancing at the clock every few minutes. I was in a desperate state. When I got home, I could neither sit down nor stand up. I couldn't watch television for longer than two minutes and I couldn't read a book, not even the *Daily Mail*. An unbearable restlessness possessed me. I could neither sleep nor relax. I was like a hunted creature with nowhere to turn, and I don't think I have ever been so unhappy.

I felt incredibly ill and tired all the time. I could hardly drag one foot after the other. It felt as if I was walking through setting concrete. I had a raging thirst which I could not slake and I seemed to spend most of my time peeing. I was overweight and my arms and legs felt unbearably heavy and I sweated an awful lot. But I still dragged myself to meetings and did not take a drink.

I told Annie all these symptoms and she looked at me thoughtfully and hard and said, 'Diabetes.' And so it turned out to be. Not a very bad case, but bad enough to require treatment. Pills and a rigid non-sugar, non-fat diet. My life was very black and if I had not had little Phoenix to comfort me, it would have been worse.

Christmas came looming up, as ever for me a time fraught with question marks and possible disaster, as well as rows and sulks and a terrible worry about money and presents. Marina offered me her house near Dublin for Christmas and said I could invite Joshua, his wife, Kitty, and their two children, Amos and Hamilton. She was going to Jamaica with her lover and children. I accepted her offer with great jubilation and once more set out for Ireland, by car. Marina's house, Pickering Forest, was only partly furnished, but it was warm and large.

The day before Christmas Kitty and I went off to visit Penny and Desmond for tea at Leixlip. We were driving up the avenue when we saw Penny coming through the trees and stopped for a few minutes to talk to her. I let Phoenix out of the car because I didn't want her peeing on Desmond's Aubusson rugs as Den had done. As Kitty started up the car, she said jokingly, 'I do hope your dog is all right,' and there was a terrible scream from under the car. Apparently Phoenix had gone to sit under the car instead of wandering about to have a pee and had been run over by the heavy back wheels. It was nobody's fault, except perhaps mine for not checking. The poor little dog was trembling and shivering in a state of shock as I leapt out of the car to rescue her, but she could not move her hindquarters and I knew at that moment she would not survive. I wrapped her up in an old coat of Desmond's and put her in front of the log fire. She was very brave and did not cry or moan and Desmond admired her bravery. We took her to the vet, but she had a ruptured spleen and a broken pelvis and various other complications, and, with a very sad and sickened heart, I held her in my arms as the vet put her down.

The next morning Joshua and I dug her grave in the rose avenue that I had pruned the summer before. It was very cold and there was a harsh wind blowing.

It was Christmas Day and we had been invited to celebrate the occasion at Leixlip. The children were excited and happy and had lots of presents. The big hall at Leixlip was full of brightly wrapped gifts and gaily dressed people all milling about and talking and laughing. I felt quite desolate, but I made a big effort to be normal and sociable. It was difficult. At lunch I was sitting next to Oliver, who on these occasions can be a great comfort. I wanted to get drunk and forget what had happened but something stopped me. Maybe it was my fellowship's teaching or God who kept me away from the alcohol, but I fell upon the brandy butter and Christmas pudding like a demon and had three helpings.

Later on we played games and chatted and gossiped. Kitty and Joshua took the children home, while Penny asked me to spend the night at Leixlip and said she had a lovely comfy bed just for me. I was feeling rather strange, somehow disassociated, and I accepted gratefully. One of the party was very, very drunk and making an utter fool of herself. At the same time she was very funny and, though it was unkind of me, I amused and distracted myself by laughing at her.

The next morning I felt very heavy and leaden and had rather a pain in my chest. Catherine Palmer, who had the bedroom next door to mine, came in and asked me if I'd like a cup of tea. I croaked, 'Yes please.' Then I fell asleep again, I don't know for how long. I didn't have my diabetic pills with me, but I didn't think about that. Dr Hanlon, the local doctor, came into my room. He did various things and then said, 'Well, Henrietta, I'm sending you off to hospital. You've got a high temperature and maybe you've had a heart attack. An ambulance is coming to fetch you.'

I was put in a wheelchair and carried down the stairs and wheeled up the passage to the front door, where the ambulance stood. Just as we got to the door I was violently sick. The ambulance klaxon was on and Joshua and Mark Palmer, who were following in a car, thought I was dying and were in a terrible state. There were two nuns in the ambulance with me and I was sick all over them.

I woke up in bed with a drip in my arm and a doctor and a nurse standing by me. They told me I was on an insulin drip and that I had pneumonia, and I told them that I had cirrhosis of the liver. So once again I found myself in an Irish hospital, surrounded by the same sort of lovable nurses and doctors. They told me I would be kept in for at least ten days and that I was a bit of an idiot. I explained about Phoenix and they seemed to understand the shock and sorrow that I had been through. Nevertheless, I was kept on insulin injections, rather than put back on pills, and I had to pretend to learn how to give myself an intramuscular injection. I thought, rather wistfully, of all the times I had given myself methedrine injections for the sheer hell of it and now I had to do it to keep alive.

Chapter Thirty-One

When I got back to London, I was lonely, especially without
Phoenix, but a really nice thing had happened to my room.
Joshua and some helpers had completely transformed it in my
absence. Gone were the rather drab magnolia walls and the
old-fashioned partition between the kitchen area and the rest
of the room. Gone were the frayed coconut matting from
Habitat and the faded curtains from Oxfam. In their place
were smart Chinese-yellow walls, papier-mâché curtains, lampshade and framed mirror above the fireplace. I also found a
lovely old, faded tapestry sofa, an intriguing Egyptian-looking
coffee table and three lots of corner shelves for books and
plates. Then on the floor there was some brand new and really
smart close-weave matting of a pattern I had long admired, a
present from Monster. It was all so new and dazzling that I
was quite overwhelmed.

The papier-mâché work had been done by an artist called
Jenny Neame, who had exhibited at Joshua and Kitty's
Crucial Gallery. It was lovely. Everything was painted in

eighteenth-century colours, red, green and gold, and the curtains looked as if they were flying in the breeze. I found my pictures and hung them all up and sat on the sofa and tried to get used to everything. It took me a couple of days. I was delighted to have this charming, transformed room. I got a red telephone and I began to feel as if I were really at home.

I was beginning to feel a bit better physically and my weekly visits to Annie helped me a lot mentally. I was no longer the tormented soul that I had been a few months earlier. I continued to go to group meetings, finding myself at a session practically every night of the week. As my physical torment lessened, I began to listen to what was being said with much more attention. I started to understand that there was a spiritual dimension to these gatherings and that the act of sitting in a room full of people all in the same boat as myself and talking honestly about it was in itself a healing process. Very, very slowly I began to get better. I no longer wanted to drink, not at all. I had thought that my life would be spent gazing into pubs and off-licence windows, yearning for the comfort of a bottle, but the idea hardly ever occurred to me.

Of course there were all the discomforts of an over-sensitive system which had for forty years been used to the great anaesthetic of alcohol. I was pathetically self-conscious just walking down the street and in talking to any but my oldest friends. I was asked to a party and found myself absolutely terrified at the idea. Heretofore in my life I had never gone to a party sober, I couldn't quite conceive of it, in fact I hadn't been to anything sober in the last few years. I was quite frightened, but went along and had a fairly good time

– it was only a fairly good party in any case. I found that as people got drunk, if I was sober, they seemed to get boring.

Beatrix said to me one day, 'Madre, I think it's time you got another dog.' Quick as a flash and without thinking I replied, 'Only if it's a dachshund.' Then I realized I must be mad. Dachshunds and I were obviously doomed. I'd had two and look what happened. Then I thought of the huge, kissable paws, the melting, brown eyes and the absurdly short legs. My heart stirred and came alive with feeling again. 'OK,' I said. 'Let's find one. I think I'd like a dog, not a bitch this time.'

Beatrix and I visited a recommended breeder and saw a little dachshund family playing with their mother. The pups were eight weeks old and they were tumbling about, rolling and snarling, squeaking and biting each other. There was one pup on top of this pile who seemed to be doing most of the tormenting and having most fun. He looked spectacular, with a shining silver coat and large black blobs.

'He's a silver dapple,' said his proud owner. 'Quite unusual.'

Beatrix said, 'He's marvellous. That's the one for you.'

I wasn't sure. He was almost too healthy and extrovert. I walked across the room and picked him up. He wriggled and squirmed. 'I'm not sure,' I said. 'Can I think about it and let you know?'

By the time we got home I had made up my mind. I wanted him. Breeders always seem to live in places near Farnborough, and so it was a couple of hours later that I telephoned, my heart in my mouth from the conviction that somebody else had called in after we had left and snapped him up. But I was in luck. I could collect him in a week. He cost two hundred and fifty pounds! 'I shall call him Max,' I said to Beatrix. 'Max, after Max Mlinaric and because there is an X in the name.'

Max and I live together extremely happily now. He was an adorable puppy, funny and energetic. He has a very good sense of humour and enjoys teasing me almost beyond endurance. He has his own little basket of toys – prized old marrow bones, battered balls missing their squeaks, an old slipper, a plastic mince pie which says 'Good Boy', and, unfortunately, a pair of once very nice, gold-embroidered sandals. We take a daily walk in the Brompton Cemetery and he enjoys chasing, but never catching, the hundreds of squirrels who live there. He is hopelessly in love with a large black Belgian sheepdog who belongs to Beatrix and who treats him with tolerant disdain.

His several friends include Posy, a little red-haired dachshund who lives just three doors away, and many other small dogs we meet in the streets. The character of Edith Grove has changed in the past few years. Some old ladies have gone and their place has been taken by young and lively people. A young actress called Sophie lives where Nanny Baines used to and she has a beautiful young female tabby cat called Tabitha, who is the last of Max's passions. They look very pretty together as their colouring is similar. Tabitha treats Max with a mixture of affection and feline high-handedness. She puts on a confusing show of flirting accessibility and then swipes her deadly claws in his direction. He adores her and tries every ploy he can to cement his love, but, alas, it is doomed. Recently Tabitha had kittens and Max was convinced that he was their father. He is much loved by all the children we meet and the other day a tiny Spanish child called him 'a wa-wa chiquito'. He has had all his injections and he is very healthy, and, except for a tiny tendency to raise his leg in other people's houses, he is most well-behaved. His bright silver colouring has darkened now, but he is a very handsome dog of almost three years old.

From the very start of our relationship I took Max to my meetings, where I would put him on his lead and tie him up to my chair leg. This made me many friends and gained him many admirers, and now he almost seems to understand what is going on.

As my recovery continued, I began to achieve a certain degree of serenity and love for others. My life started to cohere. Magically, old friends appeared and I found I was making new ones. My face lost its ghastly, swollen, baggy, purple appearance and my hair grew thicker and became shiny again. I see Annie regularly and she told me when we first met, I had only a few months to live!

At the meetings I had been watching and listening to a woman who seemed particularly friendly and sympathetic. One day, fearing rejection, I plucked up my courage and asked her if I could possibly consider her as my mentor and call on her for help any time I needed it. To my amazement, she smiled and said she would be honoured. Her name is Caryl and she has done more than anyone to make me feel safe, to give me courage in the sometimes arduous struggle to stay sober, and to make me laugh at the ridiculous vicissitudes of life.

I have so many good friends now and need never feel alone again. My relationship with both my children has improved almost beyond recognition. They are both so pleased that I do not drink.

My life has completely changed. Instead of the wild swoops up and down that characterize alcoholism I seem to maintain a steady emotional equilibrium. My relationships are stable and my word is reliable: when I commit myself to something, I will do it. I am punctual and always open letters in brown envelopes, attending to them at once. I used to use my bicycle basket as a filing cabinet for unopened letters and not so many years ago I found myself in court because I could not pay my electricity bill. Now, if I cannot pay, I face up to people directly and they seem to like it much better.

I don't lose my temper very much and I try not to blame everyone else for my faults. I say my prayers, at the foot of my bed, like a child is supposed to. I listen to what people have to say and I don't automatically take an opposite point of view. I do the same old things every day and don't get bored and long for excitements. In a way I revel in sameness. I find more love in my life: I love my friends so much and am amazed that some of them have been there for over thirty years, through all my nonsenses. Quite a lot of the time I am happy, in a quiet sort of way, and this is a great satisfaction. I find that I am much more creative. I always thought that drink fuelled the creative impulse and that it was necessary for it, but I was wrong. Writing comes much more easily to me sober, now I've stopped being frightened of it. I've changed a lot of my habits and most of the changes have been surprisingly easy. I live from day to day, sober and hopeful. My grandchildren and my dog have never seen me drunk, and I trust and pray that they never will.

READ MORE IN PENGUIN

In every corner of the world, on every subject under the sun, Penguin represents quality and variety – the very best in publishing today.

For complete information about books available from Penguin – including Puffins, Penguin Classics and Arkana – and how to order them, write to us at the appropriate address below. Please note that for copyright reasons the selection of books varies from country to country.

In the United Kingdom: Please write to *Dept. EP, Penguin Books Ltd, Bath Road, Harmondsworth, West Drayton, Middlesex UB7 ODA*

In the United States: Please write to *Consumer Sales, Penguin USA, P.O. Box 999, Dept. 17109, Bergenfield, New Jersey 07621-0120.* VISA and MasterCard holders call 1-800-253-6476 to order Penguin titles

In Canada: Please write to *Penguin Books Canada Ltd, 10 Alcorn Avenue, Suite 300, Toronto, Ontario M4V 3B2*

In Australia: Please write to *Penguin Books Australia Ltd, P.O. Box 257, Ringwood, Victoria 3134*

In New Zealand: Please write to *Penguin Books (NZ) Ltd, Private Bag 102902, North Shore Mail Centre, Auckland 10*

In India: Please write to *Penguin Books India Pvt Ltd, 706 Eros Apartments, 56 Nehru Place, New Delhi 110 019*

In the Netherlands: Please write to *Penguin Books Netherlands bv, Postbus 3507, NL-1001 AH Amsterdam*

In Germany: Please write to *Penguin Books Deutschland GmbH, Metzlerstrasse 26, 60594 Frankfurt am Main*

In Spain: Please write to *Penguin Books S. A., Bravo Murillo 19, 1° B, 28015 Madrid*

In Italy: Please write to *Penguin Italia s.r.l., Via Felice Casati 20, I–20124 Milano*

In France: Please write to *Penguin France S. A., 17 rue Lejeune, F–31000 Toulouse*

In Japan: Please write to *Penguin Books Japan, Ishikiribashi Building, 2–5–4, Suido, Bunkyo-ku, Tokyo 112*

In Greece: Please write to *Penguin Hellas Ltd, Dimocritou 3, GR–106 71 Athens*

In South Africa: Please write to *Longman Penguin Southern Africa (Pty) Ltd, Private Bag X08, Bertsham 2013*

READ MORE IN PENGUIN

A CHOICE OF NON-FICTION

The Time of My Life Denis Healey

'Denis Healey's memoirs have been rightly hailed for their intelligence, wit and charm ... *The Time of My Life* should be read, certainly for pleasure, but also for profit ... he bestrides the post war world, a Colossus of a kind' – *Independent*. 'No finer autobiography has been written by a British politician this century' – *Economist*

Far Flung Floyd Keith Floyd

Keith Floyd's latest culinary odyssey takes him to the far flung East and the exotic flavours of Malaysia, Hong Kong, Vietnam and Thailand. The irrepressible Floyd as usual spices his recipes with witty stories, wry observation and a generous pinch of gastronomic wisdom.

Genie Russ Rymer

In 1970 thirteen-year-old Genie emerged from a terrible captivity. Her entire childhood had been spent in one room, caged in a cot or strapped in a chair. Almost mute, without linguistic or social skills, Genie aroused enormous excitement among the scientists who took over her life. 'Moving and terrifying ... opens windows some might prefer kept shut on man's inhumanity' – Ruth Rendell

The Galapagos Affair John Treherne

Stories about Friedrich Ritter and Dore Strauch, settlers on the remote Galapagos island of Floreana, quickly captivated the world's press in the early thirties. Then death and disappearance took the rumours to fever pitch ... 'A tale of brilliant mystery' – Paul Theroux

1914 Lyn Macdonald

'Once again she has collected an extraordinary mass of original accounts, some by old soldiers, some in the form of diaries and journals, even by French civilians ... Lyn Macdonald's research has been vast, and in result is triumphant' – Raleigh Trevelyan in the *Tablet*. 'These poignant voices from the past conjure up a lost innocence as well as a lost generation' – *Mail on Sunday*

READ MORE IN PENGUIN

A CHOICE OF NON-FICTION

The Happy Isles of Oceania Paul Theroux

'He voyaged from the Solomons to Fiji, Tonga, Samoa, Tahiti, the Marquesas and Easter Island, stepping-stones in an odyssey of courage and toughness ... This is Paul Theroux's finest, most personal and heartfelt travel book' – *Observer*

Spoken in Darkness Ann E. Imbrie

A woman's attempt to understand how and why her childhood friend became, at twenty-five, the victim of a serial killer. 'Imbrie has created a highly original and heartbreaking narrative. The ground she covers is impressive: everything from feminist critiques of cheerleaders, the pain of mother–daughter relationships to the anomalies of the American judiciary ... awesome and inspiring' – *Time Out*

Fragments of Autobiography Graham Greene

Containing the two parts of Graham Greene's autobiography, *A Sort of Life* and *Ways of Escape*, this is an engaging, vivid and often amusing account of the author's memories of his childhood, traumatic schooldays and encounters as a writer and traveller.

The New Spaniards John Hooper

Spain has become a land of extraordinary paradoxes in which traditional attitudes and contemporary preoccupations exist side by side. The country attracts millions of visitors – yet few see beyond the hotels and resorts of its coastline. John Hooper's fascinating study brings to life the many faces of Spain in the 1990s.

The Loss of El Dorado V. S. Naipaul

Focusing on the early nineteenth century, when British occupants inflicted a reign of terror on the island's black population, V. S. Naipaul's passionate and vivid recreation of the history of Trinidad exposes the barbaric cruelties of slavery and torture and their consequences on all strata of society. 'A masterpiece' – *Sunday Telegraph*

READ MORE IN PENGUIN

BIOGRAPHY AND AUTOBIOGRAPHY

Freedom from Fear Aung San Suu Kyi

This collection of writings gives a voice to Aung San Suu Kyi, human rights activist and leader of Burma's National League for Democracy, who was detained in 1989 by SLORC, the ruling military junta, and today remains under house arrest. In 1991, her courage and ideals were internationally recognized when she was awarded the Nobel Peace Prize.

Memories of a Catholic Girlhood Mary McCarthy

'Many a time in the course of doing these memoirs,' Mary McCarthy says, 'I have wished that I were writing fiction.' 'Superb ... so heartbreaking that in comparison Jane Eyre seems to have got off lightly' – *Spectator*

A Short Walk from Harrods Dirk Bogarde

In this volume of memoirs, Dirk Bogarde pays tribute to the corner of Provence that was his home for over two decades, and to Forwood, his manager and friend of fifty years, whose long and wretched illness brought an end to a paradise. 'A brave and moving book' – *Daily Telegraph*

When Shrimps Learn to Whistle Denis Healey

The Time of My Life was widely acclaimed as a masterpiece. Taking up the most powerful political themes that emerge from it Denis Healey now gives us this stimulating companion volume. 'Forty-three years of ruminations ... by the greatest foreign secretary we never had' – *New Statesman & Society*

Eating Children Jill Tweedie

Jill Tweedie's second memoir, *Frightening People*, incomplete due to her tragically early death in 1993, is published here for the first time. 'Magnificent ... with wit, without a shred of self-pity, she tells the story of an unhappy middle-class suburban child with a monstrously cruel father, and a hopeless mother' – *Guardian*